EXPLORIN(
THE THAMES V^..._.

Kingston to Goring

EXPLORING THE THAMES VALLEY

Kingston to Goring

Tom Lawrence

With Historical Notes

COUNTRYSIDE BOOKS
NEWBURY, BERKSHIRE

Based upon the author's
Thames Valley volume
in the 'Walks for Motorists' series
originally published by Frederick Warne Ltd.

This book published 1990
© Tom Lawrence 1990

COUNTRYSIDE BOOKS
3 Catherine Road
Newbury, Berkshire

ISBN 185306 102 6

Cover photograph of Lechlade taken by John Bethell

Produced through MRM Associates Ltd., Reading
Typeset by Acorn Bookwork, Salisbury
Printed in England by J. W. Arrowsmith Ltd., Bristol

Contents

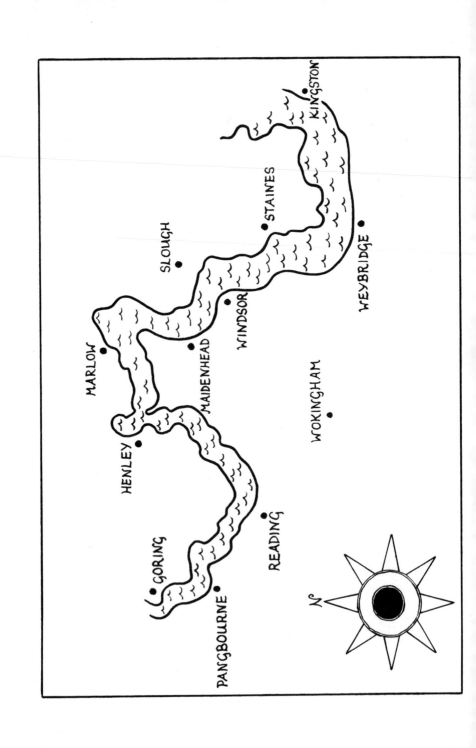

Introduction

All the walks in this book, and its companion volume, have been planned to include a section of the Thames towpath, or riverside path, in an upstream direction. Each walk is complete in itself and they need not be undertaken in any particular order. Yet the basic idea of the two books is that if you walk all 30 routes in sequence you will gain a sense of exploring the whole of the river from Kingston, on the outskirts of London, to Thames Head, its source in a Gloucestershire meadow.

With this first volume in hand, you will experience as you proceed upstream the river's gradually changing character, from suburbia to the dramatic Goring Gap.

The Thames is hemmed in by towering hills in some places; in others water meadows roll out on either side. A constant feature of every scene, however, is the endless variety of trees, forming patterns against the sky and reflecting in the water to leave a lasting memory of beauty. Yet there is much more than the environment of the river itself to be enjoyed on every one of our walks as our circular routes take us along field-paths, through woods and over the hills.

The course of the Thames has not always been the one we are about to follow. Once upon a time the river flowed into the Wash but when glacial formations in the last Ice Age pushed it south it steadily bored a way through the chalk of the Chilterns and carved the precipitous Goring Gap. Earlier still, when the North Sea was land, the Thames was but a tributary of the Rhine.

We walk with history, too. In this volume we touch Hampton Court, the great house that Cardinal Wolsey built for himself; Runnymede, where the foundations of our liberty were laid; Walton, where Caesar's invading army forded the river to do battle with the Britons; Windsor, whose great grey castle broods over two of our walks; Eton, with its noble college; Cliveden, with its echoes of politics and scandal, set in what many believe to be the most glorious stretch of the river;

and Medmenham with its memories of (maybe) aristocratic satanic orgies. We learn the origin of 'blotting his copybook', see the church which has a strange connection with the French Revolution and in which Tennyson was married, we see the graves of a famous author and a famous actress, the stretch of river on which the first Oxford and Cambridge Boat Race was rowed, and another which was known by Mr Toad, Mole and Water Rat.

Because of its unspoilt, typically English (though in no small measure, man-made) scenery the Thames has long been popular for pleasure trips. The excursions to Oxford, run by an enterprising Abingdon trader in 1555 to witness the burning at the stake of Bishops Latimer and Ridley were by no means the earliest examples of pleasure-boating on the river. Today, the constant movement of countless brightly painted pleasure craft adds colour to the enchantment of the scene.

Although the river has been navigated by barges since Saxon times, carrying goods between London and Oxford and beyond, its heyday as an artery of trade was, perhaps, in the Middle Ages. Craft were then hauled by gangs of labourers called halers, while over the long stretches that lacked a towpath vessels were pushed along by the boatmen, wielding lengthy poles. With the coming of canals in the late 18th century the river became an important navigation within the inland waterways network. The Thames and Severn Canal joined it above Lechlade in 1789, the Oxford Canal linked it to the Midlands and the North a year later, and the Basingstoke Canal which connected with the Thames through the river Wey at Weybridge was opened in 1796. Navigational improvements were then urgently demanded, particularly the provision of pound locks to replace the old 'flash' locks – dangerous, wasteful of water and ever a source of acrimony between boatmen and millers – and a continuous towpath for the horses that were now beginning to be used for drawing the vessels.

A continuous towpath was more easily demanded than provided. Although Thames Commissioners were now in charge where previously administration had been almost non-existent, there were formidable problems. The shallows, islands and muddy banks of a natural river, developments on the waterside and, not least, the intransigence of riparian owners who refused to allow a towpath on their land (or demanded exorbitant tolls if they did) all meant that a towpath had to be constructed sometimes on one bank and sometimes on the other. Numerous ferries, often with only a short distance between them, were therefore needed to take men and horses across, adding time and cost to every journey. Now that commercial traffic has died, the barges, horses and boatmen have all gone, and the ferries likewise. (We'll find a ferry, newly reinstated for passengers, on one of our rambles, though.)

The locks, of course, remain, and the cottages beside them. Whether modern or a century old these lock-keepers' residences are always pleasing in appearance while their gardens, invariably beautifully tended, are a delight to the eye when we reach them.

The National Rivers Authority (Thames Region) is responsible for the management of water resources, pollution control, land drainage, flood defences, fish stocks, conservation and much else, including recreational uses. It welcomes considerate walkers to its towpaths, as it does anglers and bird-watchers also. Not every length of towpath is a right of way but every length followed on our walks, if not a right of way, is a permissive way. Similarly, when we are walking inland from the river on our circular routes all the itineraries use public rights of way as designated on the Ordnance Survey maps with the exception of one or two paths which are permissive ways. Nevertheless, it must always be remembered that the waterside terrain and the farmland or woodland through which we go are private property and should be treated with proper respect and consideration.

The numbers of the Ordnance Survey 1:50,000 sheet, or sheets, which cover the area are given in the 'How to Get

There' section of each walk, together with the Grid Reference to enable you to pin-point the starting place. The sketch maps provided should be adequate but a full map undeniably adds interest to a walk and allows distant features to be identified.

Footwear is an important element in a walker's equipment. For most of our walks, especially those in the river's middle reaches covered by this first volume, stout shoes should, generally speaking, be adequate but boots (worn with two pairs of thick socks) are better and even wellies in wet seasons may not be out of place in certain parts.

Always interpret my directions with discretion, for paths may be diverted, hedges removed, gates dismantled, signs may disappear, and almost anything can be eroded by vandals. One of their favourite tricks, by the way, is to turn a signpost round to face the wrong way, if they can. That said, none of the rambles should present any real difficulties. The most vexing problem likely to be encountered is finding that a path across a field has been ploughed up. Or, worse, that it has not only been ploughed up but has crops growing upon it. Don't worry. Although a farmer has a right to plough a path, except for one that follows the side of a field, generally he has an obligation to make good the surface of the path within two weeks of ploughing. Unhappily, many of them are contemptuous of this duty. If you encounter a path that has been ploughed and not reinstated you may tread it out. Similarly, if the path has been planted you may walk its line through the crops, but do it in single file. Usually there is no difficulty in seeing where the line of a path runs; it is almost always straight towards the gate or stile to be seen on the opposite side of the field. Remember – if for fear of following the line of a right of way through a field of waving corn you go instead round the edge of the field, you are going where you are not supposed to go; you are trespassing, in fact.

The timings quoted in the 'Distance' section of each walk represent *my* actual walking time. You may walk faster than I do for I confess I am a fairly slow walker. You must allow extra time, of course, if you intend to visit pubs and/or churches, to picnic or loiter at locks to watch the boats go through. Many of the churches you may wish to visit you will find locked, a sad reflection upon the times we live in. I have observed, too, that it is becoming increasingly rare to find a friendly note pinned up in the porch of a church saying where the key may be obtained. Yet enquiries will generally lead to the whereabouts of the key.

A long-distance waterside route is at present being established all the way from the Thames Barrier at Greenwich to Thames Head, largely through the initiative of the Ramblers' Association. Under the auspices of the Countryside Commission the Thames Path will, it is expected, be officially opened around 1995. If you feel ready to stride out on 175 miles of lineal walking, you will need a guide entitled *The Thames Walk*, written and illustrated by the man who, since the beginning, has been the chief driving force in this admirable enterprise, David Sharp. *The Thames Walk* (new edition 1990) is published by the Ramblers' Association, price £2.95.

The circular rambles in this book, and its companion volume, will give you an enjoyable sense of exploring the Thames from Kingston to its source. Yet we do it only by taking pleasantly short samples. Our walks, on which we follow selected lengths of Thames-side paths in an upstream direction take in some of the loveliest stretches of the riverside and its surrounding glorious countryside. I have had great pleasure in preparing these walks. I hope you will gain as much enjoyment from them as I have.

Tom Lawrence
May 1990

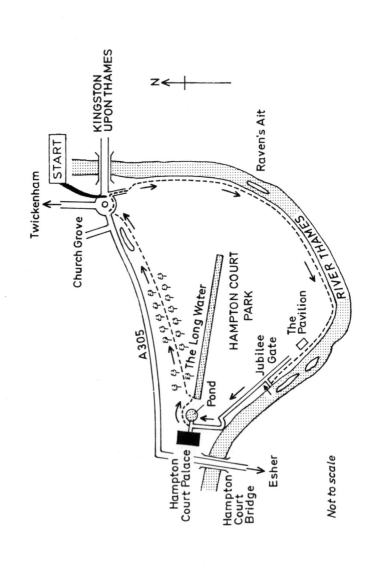

Kingston upon Thames and Hampton Court

Introduction: We have an easy walk to begin with, on much the same level all the way: along the Thames towpath, through the glorious grounds of Hampton Court Palace – with an opportunity to visit the palace if you wish – and back through a delightful royal park. For part of the way beside the river the path is shady beneath fine trees. There are wide, grassy areas rich with wild flowers and always, on the right, is Hampton Court Park with a glimpse, from time to time, of the palace in the distance.

This walk is pleasant and there are some interesting things to be seen. If you are proposing to cover the walks in this book in sequence in order to savour the ever-changing environment of the river as we progress upstream, then this first walk, starting at the very edge of Greater London, will implant a 'base' picture in your mind upon which all that follows will be built. As you walk across Kingston bridge, glance downstream, to your right. Just out of sight is Teddington lock. Up to Teddington the river is tidal, rising and falling with the motions of the sea. The river flowing beneath the bridge is therefore the first stretch of non-tidal waterway, though at the time of the high Spring tides, when the tide rises to some 2 ft over the top of Teddington weir, there can be a slight rise here, too, and as far upstream as the next lock, at Molesey.

Distance: This walk is about 4¼ miles in length, so 2½ hours should be sufficient time to complete the circuit comfortably – but add what you will for a visit to the palace and for sitting on the terrace to watch the boats go by. Be careful to start the walk in time to finish it before dusk or you will find the palace grounds locked.

Refreshments: Kingston can, of course, provide anything you may desire. At the palace there is a restaurant and a cafeteria. As you emerge from the park at the end of the walk you will find The Old King's Head just outside the gate and The White Hart across the road. Both offer bar meals and snacks. There are also at least two more pubs within a couple of minutes' walk.

How to get there: Kingston upon Thames is on the south-western edge of the Greater London area. It is well sign-posted, you will find, whether you approach on the A3, the M25, the M3 or any other road for miles around. There are numerous car parks in the town. (OS Sheet 176, GR 177 693).

The Walk: From the car park make your way (assuming you can drag yourself away from the delights of the shops!) to Kingston bridge; anybody will point you in the right direction. Cross the bridge and immediately drop down, left, to the riverside. The towpath, which from here to Hampton Court bridge is known as the Barge Walk, now lies ahead and you follow it beside the river all the way to an entrance to the grounds of Hampton Court Palace, so you can't get lost.

At first, all you can see on the other side of the water is a bewildering view of the backs of Kingston buildings, big and small, old and new. But this prospect soon changes to that of the pleasant, tree-lined Queen's Promenade at Surbiton. A striking building is St Raphael's church (1847) looking for all the world as if it had been miraculously translated from Italy.

There now appears a large island known as Raven's Ait, the site of a conference centre which won a Civic Trust award. Then, some distance further on, the route passes the richly wooded Boyle's Farm Island and at this point the prospect seems to open up, giving quite delightful views. Next comes Thames Ditton Island, recognisable by the bungalows there. Pass a private residence called The Pavilion on the right and then look out for a gate in the wall approached by flights of steps. This is Jubilee Gate, which leads into the grounds of Hampton Court Palace. If you have been walking close to the water's edge you will have to climb a bank – not very steep – to reach the gate.

Pass through the gate and turn left along a splendid terrace with the river below on the left, a close mown lawn on the right and the broad green expanse of the park beyond the lawn. At the end of the terrace, where it sweeps round to the left in a great curve, are some benches. This is perhaps the best place to sit for a while to watch the colourful traffic of pleasure boats passing up and down on the river.

When you have rested, continue round the curving terrace and then come up the broad path towards the east front of the palace. This side was designed by Sir Christopher Wren for William III. The earlier, Tudor, palace lies behind. And as you walk, the garden opens up in a breathtaking vista of brilliant colour to the right, and there is much more of it to be seen if you can spare the time to wander around.

You may wish to visit the palace, too, or find the refreshment facilities before going further.

To resume the walk, from the palace east-front entrance go towards the Great Fountain which plays in a wide circular pond in front of the entrance. Skirt the pond and then pause for a moment to lean on the iron railings to admire the impressive Long Water, a canal constructed by Charles II. Then turn left and follow an ornamental water for a short distance to an iron footbridge over it. Cross the bridge and enter, through a gate, Hampton Court Park, or 'Home Park' as it is often called.

A wide avenue of trees lies ahead and your route is straight along it, towards the tower of Kingston church which can be seen ahead in the distance. With luck, you may encounter a herd of fallow deer and you are almost certain to see the sheep which graze throughout the park. Ignore a gravelled crossing track. After a while the avenue of trees comes to an end and there is an open, green area before the trees begin again. At this point bear slightly left and make your way along the right-hand side of an elongated stretch of water called Hampton Wick Pond. There are some seats conveniently placed if you feel like a rest again.

However, you are near the end of your journey and Kingston Gate has already come within sight. Pass through the gate and turn right. Within a few minutes you will be on Kingston bridge and the town lies before you.

Historical Notes

Kingston upon Thames: Although the Royal Borough of Kingston upon Thames is noted for its splendid shops and departmental stores rather than its historical remains, it has always been a place of considerable economic and strategic importance. Its bridge (not the present one) was the first upstream from London Bridge until Putney Bridge was built in 1729. Kingston retains its character as a market town, which it has been since at least 1242. Seven 10th century kings are believed to have been crowned on the Coronation Stone which now stands outside the Guidhall. The 14th century All Saints' church, with an 18th century tower, overlooks the market place. The Museum's main exhibit tells the story of Eadweard Muybridge, the pioneer photographer of movement, who was born in Kingston in 1830 and died there in 1904.

Hampton Court Palace: King Henry VIII did not at all approve of Cardinal Wolsey, a butcher's son, getting above himself by building the largest house in England. In an optimistic, but unavailing, attempt to regain the king's favour Wolsey gave it to him. Henry enlarged it, adding the magnificent Great Hall as well as other buildings. Henry's only son, later Edward VI, was born in the palace and his mother, Henry's third wife Jane

Seymour, died there. Charles I was imprisoned there and Cromwell later moved in. Charles II loved the place. A tour of the palace includes, as well as the State Apartments, the Great Kitchen of the Tudor palace, where it is easy to conjure up a mental picture of sweating cooks preparing a multi-course feast of pies and puddings and exotic roasts for the revellers in the Great Hall 'while greasy Joan doth keel the pot'. Also to be seen is the tennis court where Henry disported himself when he was still slim and lissom. The glorious gardens of 44 acres were largely laid out in the late 17th century. Although Hampton Court is the country's grandest palace, George II was the last monarch to occupy it. Finally, there is the famous Maze. I **could** tell you the secret of how to find your way out when you seem hopelessly lost, but why should I spoil your fun?

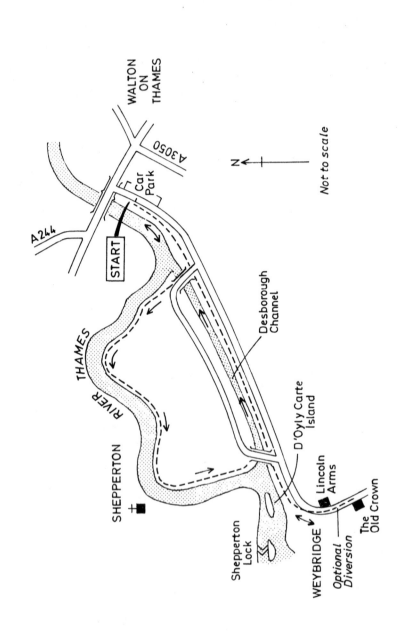

Walton-on-Thames

Introduction: This easy, short walk, on excellent paths throughout, is the only one in the book to follow water all the way. It makes an enjoyable stroll. There is an opportunity for an imaginative reader to picture, where a line of riverside bungalows now stands, a line of valiant Britons drawn up to oppose Caesar, during his second invasion in 54BC, as he forded the river with well-disciplined and fearsome forces. We see a junction of waterways, a peaceful scene today but formerly a busy place where water-borne commercial traffic converged. And, finally, we walk along a canal, dug as recently as the 1930s, but which isn't called a canal. The only thing that can mar this walk a little is that trees and bushes have grown up luxuriantly between the river and the path along quite extensive parts of the route so that our view of the river is often restricted.

Distance: The length of this ramble is only 2½ miles so 1½ hours should be sufficient – but add something, of course, if you divert into Weybridge for refreshments.

Refreshments: There are no refreshment facilities on the actual route but a short diversion may be made, two-thirds of the way along, into Weybridge where pubs serving bar meals and snacks are conveniently located. Also, during appropriate seasons of the year, a couple of vans selling ice-cream and soft drinks are usually stationed on the car park where you will leave your car. In Walton-on-Thames there are facilities of every kind.

How to get there: The free car park, the starting point of our ramble, adjoins the minor road (Walton Lane) which branches off to the left just before the 'temporary' Walton bridge; to the left, that is to say, if you approach the bridge from the Walton side, but to the right if you come across the bridge from the Shepperton side. (OS sheet 176, GR 093 663).

The Walk: Having safely parked the car, cross the road and the wide grass verge beside it to reach the towpath at just about the point where Caesar forded the river with his army. Turn left. After 5 or 6 minutes walking you come to a bridge over the Desborough Channel. Go up the slope onto the bridge and cross it. The Desborough Channel, as you will see, looks like a broad canal which, in fact, it is. At the end of the slope off the bridge, go forward – at the point where the road bends left – along a little road, by the riverside.

When this road, in turn, bends left go ahead along a tree-lined path beside the river. There are playing fields to the left and, later, a pleasant open space spreads out. This, a sign informs us, is the Surrey County Council's Point Meadow. Soon, the tower of the 'new' Shepperton church comes into view across the river; 'new' because it was built as recently as 1613 to replace an earlier church which was washed away during floods. Should you wish to take a trip over to Shepperton as an 'optional extra', an enjoyable crossing can be made by the ferry, newly established, which you will shortly reach if you divert towards Weybridge. The ferry runs hourly on the hour on weekdays from 8am to 5.30pm; every half hour on Saturdays 9am to 5.30pm and every half-hour on Sundays 10am to 5.30pm.

The Thames and its towpath meander round Point Meadow in a great curve known as the Halliford Bend, a favourite spot of Isaac Walton's, of *The Compleat Angler* fame. For a while the path runs a little way inland but soon comes back near the water's edge. But when the path bears left to climb a gentle slope to an iron gate, follow it, for here is the bridge over the

Desborough Channel where it rejoins the river. A plaque on the bridge was unveiled on 10th July 1935 by the Rt Hon Lord Desborough, KG, GCVO, Chairman of the Conservators, and records that the work had been commenced in 1930 with financial aid from the Surrey and Middlesex County Councils.

On the far side of the bridge turn right down a steep flight of steps to the towpath where the walk continues under the bridge and beside the Channel. However, if you wish to make an optional diversion into Weybridge, carry on the other way for a few hundred yards. You will pass D'Oyly Carte Island, which was the summer residence of Richard D'Oyly Carte, the producer of the Gilbert and Sullivan Operas at the Savoy Theatre in London from 1877 onwards. The imaginative reader will readily conjure up a mental vision of the gaiety, laughter and song which erupted here when the entire opera company was invited to this romantic spot each summer and lavishly entertained with food and wine.

Just beyond the island, which is linked to the shore by an elegant footbridge, the river widens at Shepperton lock and here is the ferry above mentioned, reinstated after a lapse of many years. A few yards further along the towpath you are obliged to bear left onto a road beside the Wey Navigation, which flows into the Thames just here. From this point, the southernmost on the Thames, the river was once linked, by navigation and canal, to the South Coast. What you probably had in mind when you diverted to Weybridge now materialises: The Lincoln Arms is on the left while The Old Crown, an attractive weather-boarded inn, lies just round the bend in the road.

The walk proper, however, continues along the Desborough Channel. Although it is fairly straight and, like all canals, probably presented a stark gash across the countryside when it was constructed, kindly Nature now presents a prospect by no means unattractive. The fine trees on the opposite bank have all grown, presumably, in the interim. This side is pleasant enough, too, apart from the occasional noise of passing traffic on the parallel road, on the other side of which lies Oatlands Park, where once stood a palace which Henry VIII built for his fourth wife, Anne of Cleves, largely with material from demolished monasteries.

At the end of the Desborough Channel, you will pass under the bridge which you crossed near the beginning of the walk and your final few steps duplicate your outward progress. Ahead is Walton bridge. Before you reach it, however, you will have reached your car.

Historical Notes

Julius Caesar: Near the starting point of the ramble, above Walton bridge, is where it is believed that Caesar, with his army, forded the river in 54BC during his second invasion. He was in pursuit of Cassivellaunus, a British chief of the tribes living north of the Thames who had enjoyed some brief successes over the Romans. But once Caesar had forced a passage over the Thames the Briton was put to flight. Cassivellaunus eventually sued for peace, which was granted in return for hostages and a yearly tribute. Caesar wrote an account of the battle, saying that the bank had been planted with sharp stakes, and similar stakes were embedded beneath the water. One of these stakes, found in the river in 1777 when the water was exceptionally low, may be seen in the British Museum.

Walton Bridge: There has been more than one bridge here since the first was completed in 1750. A wooden structure, it had become ruinous by 1780, although not before Canaletto had recorded it on canvas. It was replaced by a stone and brick structure which Turner painted, but in 1859 a great storm swept away part of it and an iron bridge was erected in its place. By 1954 this had become unsafe and the 'temporary' bridge – which is still in use – was put up beside it.

Walton-on-Thames: Although the town's history can be traced back to Saxon times, and some evidence of the Saxon building may be discerned in the present church of St Mary, there is not a great deal of historical interest in the town, pleasant as it is. A 'scold's' bridle, formerly a favourite instrument of punishment for nagging women, is exhibited in the church. There is a monument to Viscount Shannon, who died in 1740, by Louis Roubiliac, one of the most eminent of 18th century sculptors.

William Lilley, a 17th century astrologer, lived in the town, as did Sir Arthur Sullivan, of Gilbert and Sullivan fame; President Bradshaw, who was one of the judges who signed the death warrant of King Charles I; and Cecil Hepworth, who opened one of the first film studios in England around the turn of the century. The author's father, who lived in Walton as a boy (his father being stationmaster) appeared in one of Hepworth's first pictures. With several other boys he was engaged to run behind a horse-drawn water cart, which sprayed water on the roads in those days to keep down the dust. The boys were directed to attempt to cling on to the back of the cart, whereupon the water was turned on, drenching them. That was the whole scenario. The boys each received a fee of 6*d*.

The Wey Navigation: The river Wey was one of the first to be canalised, to Guildford in the 1650s and to Godalming in 1764. The Wey and Arun Junction Canal, opened in 1823 from near Guildford, joined the river Arun which in turn flowed into the sea at Littlehampton. The canal fell into disuse before the end of the century but, until it did, the Thames at Weybridge was linked to the English Channel.

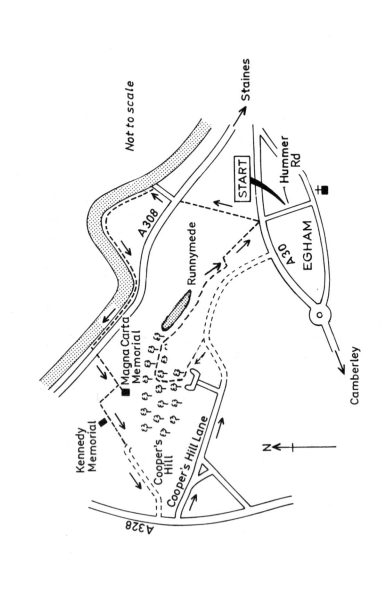

Not to scale

Staines

Hummer Rd

START

A308

Runnymede

A30

EGHAM

Camberley

Magna Carta Memorial

Kennedy Memorial

Cooper's Hill

Cooper's Hill Lane

A328

N

Runnymede

Introduction: Runnymede clearly demands a place in our book, not only as one of the most notable sites beside the Thames but as one of the most famous in all England. In fact, the walk is something of an experience, for not only do we tread on a meadow steeped in history but also on a patch of soil that is, literally, American and – on a hill top – on holy ground. Although it is not long, our walk is moderately strenuous in that there is a hill to be climbed (but the view from the top is worth it). Parts may be very wet in winter or after heavy rain, I was told by a local resident who said that wellies would not then be out of order.

Distance: A circuit of some 4½ miles, for which 2½ hours should be enough, including a visit to the Air Forces Memorial.

Refreshments: There are no facilities on the actual route but a short diversion may be made to a cafeteria near the Kennedy Memorial.

How to get there: The starting point is Egham, a small town just west of Staines and by-passed by the A30. There are two or three car parks, the most convenient being in Hummer Road, a residential road running to the left of The Catherine Wheel, almost opposite the church. Note, however, that the maximum stay in this car park is 4 hours. (OS sheet 176, GR 012 716).

The Walk: Walk down Hummer Road, cross the busy A30 carefully and take the clear asphalt path across part of Runnymede. Cross the A308 and go down narrow Yard Mead, opposite, to the river and turn left along the towpath. When the riverside bungalows soon come to an end keep near the water as the river sweeps round on a curve to the left and then right. The other side of the river is deeply wooded while on this side there is a recreational park. On the next stretch the river is sometimes hidden from view by trees and bushes that have grown up along the water's edge.

Ignore a footpath sign beside a stile you will notice on the other side of the road. Carry on, as close to the river as possible, until you come to a small parking area – then cross the road and go over the meadow to the temple-like Magna Carta Memorial which can be plainly seen ahead. Erected by the American Bar Association it commemorates the granting of Magna Carta, a 'symbol of freedom under law' in these meadows in 1215. The exact spot where the reluctant King John put pen to parchment is unknown.

After visiting the memorial, turn left outside the gate and make your way along the meadow, past an oak tree planted by the Queen in 1987 to mark National Tree Week, and, with the hedge on your left, come to the entrance to the John F Kennedy Memorial. At this point a short diversion may be made, if desired, half right over the meadow, to the cafeteria in one of the red and white lodges.

Follow the winding path and steps up Cooper's Hill towards the Kennedy Memorial. Simple, yet impressive, it stands on 'an acre of English ground . . . given to the United States of America by the people of Britain' in memory of a president who died by an assassin's hand.

Continue on the path climbing up the hill behind, and to the left of, the memorial. The path becomes a drive and rises ahead, with the glorious park-like grounds of the Shoreditch College of Brunel University to the left, to the A328. On reaching the road, turn left, keeping to a rough path on the wide grass verge. You very soon leave the road, however, by turning left into Cooper's Hill Lane.

The Air Forces Memorial, reached after 10 minutes' walking along the lane, should be visited not so much for the superb views, especially from the tower, as for a deeply moving experience.

On leaving the memorial, turn left. The lane bends left and becomes a track, then bends right. Here, go left along a footpath by a National Trust sign saying 'Cooper's Hill Slopes'. When the path soon divides, take the main, right fork and enter a most pleasant, woodland area. Keep ahead as the path drops downhill, veers right, then left and twists and turns until eventually a stile is reached. Cross this, ignore another stile on the left and go forward on the path ahead. But be careful!

After a few paces, a less distinct path goes off right (opposite a five-bar gate) across a sloping field, slightly leftwards, towards some trees. The path carries on, along the right-hand side of the trees and when they come to an end you will see the elongated Langham Pond. Make your way beside it, the water to your left, cross a stile and continue your direction. Soon after the path strays a little way from the pond a stile will be seen on the left, leading to a wooden bridge over a ditch. Cross this, and you are back beside the water. The path soon merges with a path coming from a stile in the hedge on the right. Bear left with this path – and make your way across the meadow, heading for the top of Hummer Road which is mid-way along the row of houses ahead.

Historical Notes

Magna Carta, the Great Charter of English liberties, was presented to King John by his barons at Runnymede on 15th June 1215. It enshrined the conception that there are laws and customs in England which even monarchs must respect. After nine days of arguing the king agreed to remedy his barons' complaints and set his seal upon the document. A few altera-

tions were subsequently made but the final version was con-
firmed by Edward I in 1297. Since then, it has formed the basis
of the constitutions and statutes of many other countries,
including the United States of America.

The Air Forces Memorial, opened by the Queen in 1953, was
designed by Sir Edward Maufe, RA. It is a beautiful place,
impeccably kept and inexpressibly sad. Carved on its cloister
walls are 20,455 names of those who lost their lives while
serving with the Air Forces of the Commonwealth in opera-
tions from bases in the UK and north-west Europe during the
Second World War, and who have no known grave. In her
address, Her Majesty quoted the curiously prophetic lines of
the poet, Alexander Pope, referring to the hill upon which the
memorial stands:

'On Cooper's Hill eternal wreaths shall grow
While lasts the mountain, or while Thames shall flow.'

Eton and Boveney Lock

Introduction: This is an easy, enjoyable walk. The stretch beside the Thames is very attractive, there are some interesting things to see, it is all on the same level and no difficulties are likely to arise. A few steps at the beginning and end of the walk duplicate Walk Five.

Distance: This ramble covers some 4 miles, so 2 hours should be more than sufficient.

Refreshments: There are no facilities on the actual route but at almost exactly the mid-point a diversion of only a few yards may be made into Eton where there are pubs and restaurants.

How to get there: The starting point is near the hamlet of Boveney which is reached along a minor road running south from the B3026 as it crosses Dorney Common on its way from Eton to Taplow (near which it intersects the A4). By Boveney Court Farm the road bends sharply left (Lock Path) and it should be possible to park on a patch of fairly rough grass a little further on to the right and just short of a much larger patch of grass reserved as a parking space for an angling club. (OS sheet 175, GR 938 778).

The Walk: The walk starts by continuing along Lock Path, ignoring a path, right, which leads to the chapel of St Mary Magdalene, and pass through a gate leading to an avenue of fine chestnut trees. When the trees end and the lane bears right to Boveney Lock, go ahead on a bridleway (not signposted) at

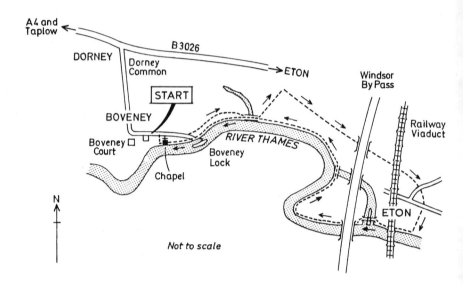

the right-hand side of a field. This bridleway eventually leads right through a gap in the hedge and comes to the riverside at a small, concrete bridge over a stream.

Cross the bridge and immediately turn half-left along a bridleway through the middle of a field – in other words, keep to an angle of about 45 degrees to the towpath. When a crossing track is met, turn right, heading slightly to the left of Windsor Castle, ahead, and towards the five elegant arches beneath the busy Windsor by-pass road. The great grey edifice of the castle is a grand sight to contemplate as you make your way over the field. Another interesting feature as you approach the arches is the contrast between their modern style and that of the arches of the 19th century railway viaduct to be seen between them.

Pass beneath the by-pass and your path now continues in the direction of Eton College chapel. On the other side of the impressive railway viaduct, which seems more suited to Queen Victoria's royal train than the two-car diesel sets that cross it today, your way lies half-right over a playing field (the path actually starts a few feet to the left) to a gap in the hedge. Through this, go left along a good path at the left-hand edge of another playing field. (These are not the playing fields on which the Battle of Waterloo was won!)

Go over a narrow, but busy, road to a small gate opposite and cross another field, now heading at first just to the right of the castle. On reaching a small car park, immediately turn right and cross a road to a stile and make your way, leftish, over the field to the Thames and turn right along the towpath.

Pass beneath a railway bridge, over two iron footbridges and under the by-pass – and the best part of the walk begins. Stay beside the river; ignore the wide cycleway running ahead. This attractive reach of the river is broad and wooded. As it sweeps round in a sharp right-hand bend, notice an iron post scored by the towlines of horse-drawn barges many years ago.

A wooden footbridge takes you over a backwater of the river; the two iron footbridges you crossed earlier were at the other end of it. The next bridge you come to, some way further along, will be the little concrete one crossed when the route touched the riverside near the beginning of the walk. Before reaching it, however, notice a seat donated by Eton College and a stone bearing a plaque, some of the wording on which will probably be comprehensible only to Eton scholars. 'Bathing Regulations at Athens' it is headed, and one of the regulations is 'Boys who are undressed must either get at once into the water or get behind screens when boats containing ladies come in sight.'

After crossing the concrete bridge, carry on along the towpath. There are bushes on either side until you come to Boveney Lock, a particularly charming spot, I'm told, at lilac time, but a pleasant spot at any time, to watch the boats going through. Go past the lock, along the towpath to the tiny riverside chapel of St Mary Magdalene, turn right onto the path to the left of the chapel and soon come to the parking place where, a little to the left, you left your car.

Historical Notes

Eton: Eton College, which today has well over 1,000 scholars, was founded 'for 24 poor and indigent scholars' by Henry VI in 1440. The chapel, begun a year later, is the oldest building and the king initially intended it to be twice as long. The Lower School, built in 1445, is the original schoolroom. The college has continued to grow over the centuries so that many periods are represented in its buildings.

The chapel contains some early wall paintings, dating from the 15th century, behind the choir stalls. The paintings were covered by whitewash during the Reformation but were exposed again in 1923. Several windows, destroyed by a bomb in 1940, have been replaced; eight are by John Piper. The chapel is open every afternoon, as are the school yard and cloisters and there are guided tours during the summer.

The 4th June is Eton's big day when, in celebration of the birthday of George III, a procession of boats is rowed down the river by boys in picturesque costumes. The day, which is also speech day, ends with a grand firework display.

Eton's narrow, but charming, High Street leads down to the pedestrian-only bridge into Windsor.

Windsor: The Guidhall, begun in 1686, was completed by Sir Christopher Wren. A tale is told that when the townsfolk saw that Wren had provided no central supporting pillars they insisted that pillars should be put in lest, they feared, the floor above would sag. Wren obliged – but to prove his architectural competence, he left a gap between the top of each pillar and the ceiling. The gaps can still be seen.

Windsor Castle dominates the town and the countryside around. Although it enshrines nearly a thousand years of British history, much of the castle is, actually, not all that old. Tremendous alterations and additions were carried out by Charles II, George III, George IV (who spent well over £1 million, a lot of money in those days) and Queen Victoria. In fact, much of the exterior, as well as the upper part of Henry II's great Round Tower, is 19th century, the work of an architect named Wyatville, who was responsible for demolishing many of the older parts of the castle. Nothing of the original Norman remains.

The American tourist who wanted to know why the castle had been built so near the airport had noticed (as you will not fail to notice, too) the endless stream of aircraft climbing out of Heathrow. It is not hard to understand why Windsor Castle is the Queen's least favourite residence!

The castle precincts are open daily but the State Apartments are open only when the Queen is not in residence. St George's Chapel was completed by Henry VIII. In the colourful choir are the stalls of the Knights of the Garter, the highest order of knighthood in the world, instituted, it is believed, by Edward III about 1348. Above the stalls are the knights' swords, helmets, mantles and banners. In a vault below the chapel rest the remains of Henry VIII and his wife Jane Seymour, Charles I and one of Queen Anne's many children. At the west end is the tomb of King George V and Queen Mary while in the Albert Memorial Chapel lie George III, George VI and William IV with other royalty.

St Mary Magdalene Chapel, Boveney: Parts of the chapel are 12th century. The origins of this tiny structure, with its weather-boarded bell turret, are obscure. Perhaps it was used by bargees and other rivermen when there was a busy wharf nearby for the transhipping of timber from Windsor Forest. It is also said that it may have been at one time a chapel of ease for the neighbouring house, Boveney Court, once owned by the Abbey of Burnham. Services are held occasionally in this lonely, but well cared for place of worship. Although it is locked the key may be obtained.

Dorney

Introduction: There is a nice long stretch of the river to be followed on this walk, and a very attractive stretch it is, too. The paths throughout are good and no difficulties are likely to be encountered. We can visit one of the finest Tudor manor houses in England at Dorney Court and an utterly fascinating old church which seems miraculously to have been overlooked by 19th century restorers. We shall walk on an ancient common, something out of a past age, where cattle and sheep roam where they will (including on the road). We catch a glimpse of Dracula's castle and discover how Windsor Castle dominates the landscape for miles around.

This walk may be combined with Walk Six.

Distance: This walk covers about 5½ miles – or a little bit less if you take a short cut to avoid a few yards that duplicate Walk Four; 2½ hours should be sufficient for the actual walking.

Refreshments: The only place for refreshments on the circuit is The Palmers Arms which offers – according to the board outside – 'Spirited Food' and this hostelry is located not far from the starting (or finishing) point of our ramble.

How to get there: Dorney, your starting point, is an attractive village on the B3026, the road from Eton to just north of Taplow. It intersects the A4 at a roundabout. Near the west end of the village a minor road, signposted 'Dorney Reach', turns off. Take this road and park discreetly, perhaps on a patch of rough ground just before the road bends sharp right, a little way past St James' church. There is room for four or five

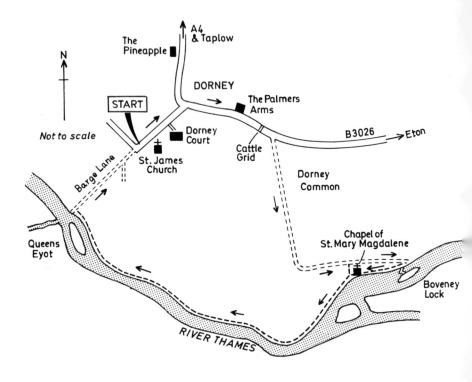

cars. Actually, you may have difficulty in spotting the church as it is grouped with Dorney Court and lies partly hidden by buildings. (OS sheet 175, GR 924 790).

The Walk: Begin by turning around on yourself and going back along the road towards Dorney village. You may care to visit the church first, however, as it is very interesting. Before you come to the end of the road there is yet another attraction: an entry to the splendid Dorney Court. It is open, during the summer, on certain days only (see Historical Notes) so one must hope you have picked one of the right days!

For the walk cross the road at the T-junction, turn right and make your way through Dorney village, passing The Palmers

Arms on the left and then, on the right, what must surely be one of the few Tudor petrol filling stations and motor repair workshops anywhere. But Dorney, as you will have observed, is rich in lovely old Tudor buildings.

Having crossed a cattle grid you are on Dorney Common. After passing a farm entrance on the right you will find a path on the common running parallel with the road and a few yards from it. This soon curves round to the right; follow it round, now parallel with a little road signposted 'Boveney'. Even when the path peters out you can still walk on the grass, if you wish. Windsor Castle becomes visible in the distance.

At Boveney Court Farm turn left along Lock Path. At the end of the piece of rough ground which serves as a parking place for the exclusive use of members of an angling society you will see, away to the right, the entrance to a footpath. It will bring you past the tiny chapel of St Mary Magdalene. If you have already done Walk Four, turn right here and skip the next paragraph. But the short cut will not shorten the walk by very much and you will miss an attractive part of it, including Boveney Lock, if you have not already seen it.

So, for the full walk, go forward over a cattle grid and along a beautiful avenue of chestnut trees and come to Boveney Lock. After pausing for a while to watch a variety of craft going up or down through this picturesque lock, turn right along the towpath and come to the isolated chapel.

Two miles or so of wholly pleasant riverside walking, with wide open country on the right and the river on the left, lie ahead on a path which, although sometimes narrow, is always good. Eton College boathouse, soon reached, is modern but of unusual design and a considerable feature. After a while there comes into view on the other side of the water a quite remarkably exotic castellated building. This is Oakley Court which has featured in several films, doing duty as both Dracula's castle and St Trinian's school. Later again, you come abreast of a large wooded island. This is known as Queen's Eyot and it belongs to Eton College.

Soon after passing the end of the eyot you will see a path leading off from the towpath, opposite Bray Marina. To complete the walk turn right along this path. (However, if you are combining this walk with Walk Six, do not turn right but carry on along the towpath and pick up the itinerary from the fourth paragraph of 'The Walk' section of Walk Six.)

This path is called Barge Lane and as you travel along it you can see, again, away across the vast field to the right, the ever-dominating pile of Windsor Castle. When a track joins from the right, carry on ahead and in a couple of hundred yards or so you will come out on the road by the side of which you left your car.

Do visit St James' church if you didn't before setting out.

Historical Notes

Dorney Court: There are few finer Tudor manor houses anywhere. It is still the home of the Palmer family, in which it has been handed down from generation to generation since 1600. The house has changed little since the 16th century; a kingpin in the roof bears the date 1510 but some of the construction is earlier still. With its many gables, its mellow brick and ancient timber and distinctively Tudor tall chimneys, the house seems to dream of days long gone. Inside are some fine furniture, beautiful panelling and a priest's hiding hole reminding us of those terrible times when a Catholic priest, if discovered, faced hanging, drawing and quartering. The house is open at Easter weekend and then on Sundays until the 2nd Sunday in October and on Sundays, Mondays and Tuesdays from June until the end of September, from 2pm to 5.30pm. It is said that a gardener at Dorney Court grew the first pineapple in England and presented it to Charles II. Hence the name of another pub in the village, The Pineapple, which we shall encounter on the next ramble. The entrance to Dorney Court for cars (there is free parking) is opposite The Palmers Arms.

St James' Church, Dorney: Of flint construction and with a 16th century brick tower, the church has an air, unlike the majority of churches, of having stayed unchanged for many years and it even seems to have been spared Victorian restoration. It is lit by 17th century candelabra and well worth seeing are the high-sided family pew, 400 years old, and a tremendous monument and tomb of a 16th century knight and his wife. Their 15 children are represented on it, too; some of them are carrying skulls in their hands which apparently indicates which of them were dead at the time the monument was erected. Some wall paintings, probably of the 14th century, are to be seen on either side of the entrance to the north chapel in which the great monument stands. At the west end, the 17th century gallery is still intact. It is balustraded and of excellent, though simple workmanship. Some of the pews are 17th century work, too. The font, which is late Norman, is large. All in all, it is – as I am sure you will agree – an utterly unspoilt, charming old church. Only the Alternative Service Books seem to strike an incongruous note. If the church is locked the key may be obtained.

St Mary Magdalene Chapel, Boveney: See notes at the end of Walk Four.

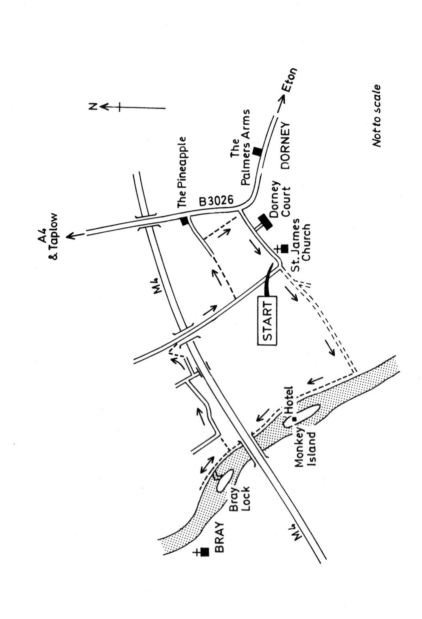

N

A4
& Taplow

M4

The Pineapple

B3026

The Palmers Arms

Dorney Court

DORNEY

Eton

St.James Church

START

Hotel

Monkey Island

Bray Lock

BRAY

M4

Not to scale

Bray Lock

Introduction: The star attraction on this easy walk is picturesque Bray lock, one of the loveliest on the Thames and one
which, not surprisingly, won the Lock Garden Competition
many times when the yearly contest for lock-keepers was run.
This stretch of river is very attractive and, if you are willing to
add an extra couple of miles or so, you can see a most
interesting example of industrial archaeology. This is the
Maidenhead railway bridge, a creation of that Victorian genius
Isambard Kingdom Brunel, with a wider span for a brick
bridge than any other in the world.

This walk may be combined with Walk Five.

Distance: The circuit is about 3½ miles, so rather less than 2
hours should be sufficient. But add something, of course, if you
take the optional extension to Maidenhead railway bridge.

Refreshments: Ice creams, soft drinks, crisps and the like may
be purchased at Bray Lock. Otherwise the only refreshment
place is The Pineapple pub, and that lies a short distance off
the actual route, but is conveniently near the end of the
journey.

How to get there: The starting point is near St James' church in
Dorney, an attractive village rich in Tudor buildings. It lies on
the B3026 that runs from Eton to join the B476 near Taplow
and which intersects the A4 at a roundabout. In Dorney
village, turn into the minor road signposted 'Dorney Reach'
and park discreetly, perhaps on the patch of rough ground near

41

where the road bends sharply right. This is the same starting point as for the previous walk and there is room for four or five cars there. (OS Sheet 175, GR 924 790).

The Walk: By the sharp bend, go along Barge Lane, a stony lane at a 'Public Footpath and Bridleway' sign. At the fork, keep right. A pleasant walk to the riverside lies ahead. On the left is the vast Thames Field and, shortly, a glance over your left shoulder will reveal the great grey pile of Windsor Castle in the distance. On reaching the towpath, turn right.

Before long you will pass Monkey Island. The way here is garden-like; the grass is mown and there are houses, lying back from the riverside, calculated to test to the uttermost one's adherence to the Tenth Commandment. Then, suddenly, all is changed and, through a white, wooden swing-gate you will find yourself on a path among the trees of a small wood.

Soon you will pass beneath the bridge carrying the noisy M4 motorway across the river. Over there lies the village of Bray and if you later go on as far as Maidenhead railway bridge you may catch a glimpse over the trees of the tower of 13th century St Michael's church, where the famous Vicar of Bray was parson. But it is a long walk from here to the village so it is better to visit it by car after completing the walk.

And so you come to Bray Lock. Just before reaching it, however, notice a wide gravel path leading away from the towpath. After visiting the lock you will come back and take this path. But don't neglect to take the few paces forward to see the lock at close quarters and maybe rest there for a while to watch the colourful pageant of boats going through. Walk a little way past the lock, too, for its most enchanting display of lawns and flowers, an explosion of colour on the upstream side. And, of course, if you wish to see the Maidenhead railway bridge, continue along the towpath, but you must return the same way.

Go back to the path you noticed before you reached the lock and turn along it. It soon comes out into a lane at a corner, where you proceed ahead. At a T-junction of lanes, by a house called Rookwood, turn right. The lane is rudely cut off not far ahead by the M4, so it is necessary to turn left just short of the motorway along a private road at a 'No Cycling' sign. At the end of this road you will come to a zig-zag path which brings you up onto a bridge over the busy road. Cross the bridge, cross the road and carry on along it.

Opposite a row of white terraced houses you will find a foot-path sign by a stile on the left. This is your route. The path goes across a field to a stile on the other side of it. Cross the stile, a footbridge over a ditch and another stile. The path then goes up the left-hand side of a field to another stile and then by the side of another field to a stile leading into a cart-track.

At this point, hestitate. If you go over the stile and up the cart-track for a short distance you will come to The Pineapple, a 'real ale' pub whose name commemorates the first growing of a pineapple in England at nearby Dorney Court during Charles II's reign.

To continue your walk, however, turn right through 90 degrees and continue along the left-hand side of a field with a barbed wire fence on the left. Eventually, you will come to a stile leading into Court Lane. Turn right in the lane and soon you will reach the corner near which you left your car. But before getting there you will pass a pedestrian and coach entrance to Dorney Court; the entrance for cars (and the free car park) is round the corner behind you, in the village and opposite The Palmers Arms. Then comes the wonderful St James' church. There is some information about both these places of interest in the notes at the end of the previous walk. Do visit the church before going home; it's fascinating.

Historical Notes

Monkey Island: The name is a corruption of Monk's Eyot (or Eye or Ey) because this was monastery land. The island has had associations with royalty and nobility for centuries. Part of

43

the hotel on the island is quite old, having been built as a fishing lodge for the 3rd Duke of Marlborough, possibly to designs by Vanbrugh, the architect of Blenheim Palace. Inside may be seen paintings by an 18th century French artist named Clermont which depict monkeys dressed in the flamboyant garb of fashionable ladies and gentlemen of the day. It is a general satirical comment on contemporary goings-on.

Maidenhead railway bridge: Isambard Kingdom Brunel, that towering genius of Victorian engineers, was born in 1806 and died in 1859. During that comparatively short lifetime he built the Hungerford suspension bridge; docks at Plymouth, Milford Haven and elsewhere; the *Great Western* (the first steamship to cross the Atlantic regularly), the *Great Britain* (the first large ship to be constructed of iron and to have a screw propeller – she is now on view, partially restored, in Bristol where she was built), and the even bigger *Great Eastern*. His chief claim to fame, however, is his construction of the entire works of the Great Western Railway to which he was appointed Engineer in 1833. One of Brunel's most daring works was the Maidenhead bridge. Built in the late 1830s of brick, it has the two widest and flattest spans for brick bridges in the world; each is 128 ft wide with a rise of a mere 24 ft. When one sees the tiny train in Turner's famous picture *Rain, steam and speed*, which features this bridge, and compares the weight of that engine and wooden carriages with the great diesel locomotives and steel coaches that thunder across it today one wonders if Brunel, visionary that he was, foresaw what the future held and built accordingly. Try talking to yourself when underneath the bridge; it has a most curious echo and is known as the 'sounding arch'.

Bray: The famous Vicar of Bray might not recognise his church today for it was greatly reconstructed – at enormous expense – in the 1870s, that time of enthusiastic restoration which St James' church at Dorney was so fortunate to escape. It contains some fine old brasses and an alabaster monument with effigies of the founder of the nearby Jesus Hospital. There is also a long list of benefactions, some of which are still operative. The famous vicar, the hero of the popular ballad, was probably Simon Aleyn. He was appointed vicar in the time of Henry VIII who broke with Rome and declared himself Head of the Church in England. By changing his views during Henry's reign and during those of subsequent sovereigns, Aleyn was twice a Roman Catholic and twice an Anglican.

> '. . . I will maintain
> Unto my dying day, Sir,
> That whatsoever King shall reign
> I will be the Vicar of Bray, Sir!'

We, who have never watched heretics burnt at the stake as Aleyn did, in nearby Windsor, should hold our peace. There is another Vicar of Bray story, about a later vicar. This concerns Charles II who was returning from hunting in Windsor Forest and got separated from his entourage, lost his road and came to Bray. It was already dark when he called at the vicarage and asked for assistance. But as he had no money – Royalty never carry cash, even today – the vicar called him an impostor and turned him out of the house with great rudeness. The curate, however, who was with the vicar, said he pitied the traveller and lent him a little money. Whereupon the king revealed his identity and, upbraiding the vicar for his inhumanity, said, 'The Vicar of Bray shall be Vicar of Bray still, but the Curate shall be Canon of Windsor.' The king kept his word.

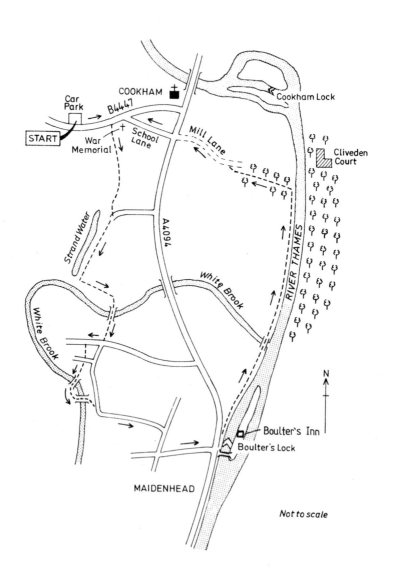

Car Park

B4447

COOKHAM

Cookham Lock

START

War Memorial

School Lane

Mill Lane

Cliveden Court

Strand Water

A4094

White Brook

RIVER THAMES

White Brook

Boulter's Inn

Boulter's Lock

MAIDENHEAD

N

Not to scale

Cliveden Reach

Introduction: An easy and interesting ramble. It begins at Cookham and later follows the breathtakingly beautiful Cliveden Reach. This is regarded by many as the loveliest part of the river. And there is Boulter's Lock on our route, too, which is often described as the most famous on the Thames. We enjoy a grand view of Cliveden Court, the great house set 200 ft above the river. Older ramblers will at once remember 'the Cliveden Set'. It was the home of the Astors; Nancy, Lady Astor, was the first woman Member of Parliament. The house and the magnificent gardens and woodlands now belong to the National Trust but the house is let as an hotel although three rooms are open to the public, as are the grounds. Unfortunately, they are all on the other side of the water!

Distance: This ramble is about 5½ miles in length so 3 hours should be sufficient for the actual walking.

Refreshments: Cookham has numerous pubs, restaurants and tea-rooms. On the the island at Boulter's Lock, half-way round the circuit, is Boulter's Inn where bar meals and snacks may be obtained. At the appropriate time of year ice cream/cold drinks vans are also on the island as well as on the car park where we start and finish our walk.

How to get there: The starting point of the walk is the small, free car park on Cookham Moor. Cookham village lies on the A4094 which runs north from Maidenhead to Bourne End, and is not quite 3 miles from Maidenhead bridge. Cookham Moor is reached by turning west onto the B4447 in the village and the car park will be found on the right-hand side a short distance past the last of the houses. (OS Sheet 175, GR 893 853).

The Walk: Start by turning left out of the car park towards Cookham village but before reaching the war memorial cross the grass on the right towards a footpath sign opposite a thatched house. This indicates your way – a path to the right of the house. The path has trees on the left and, on the right, a wall which soon gives place to railings, revealing a wide, open view.

The path bends right after a while, with the railings, and comes to a stile. It then continues, with railings still on the right, along the edge of a field and reaches another stile. Beyond this, cross a drive and carry on along a very pleasant path ahead at the right-hand edge of a field. Soon you will be walking beside an elongated pond called Strand Water and you stay beside this as you leave the field and enter the next.

At the end of this field the path divides, the right fork going across a small footbridge and the left fork – the route you must take – running along the left-hand edge of another field, with iron railings on the left. All these railings struck me as being rather an unusual feature in an agricultural environment like this. Top marks, by the way, to the farmer (or farmers) around here, and our thanks to them, for leaving the footpaths undisturbed by ploughing, unlike some of their brethren elsewhere.

Beyond another stile the path bears right to run near the right-hand edge of a field which is National Trust property. The path is only faintly visible on the ground but that does not matter; just keep near the hedge and come to a narrow footbridge over White Brook before reaching a stile. The path carries on through the middle of a field heading directly towards the spire of a Maidenhead church in the distance. At the end of the field, by a double footpath sign, you will reach an iron stile of an unusual pattern I have never seen before; but redundant, because one can walk round it. Here turn right along a track.

The track meets a wide, stony and sandy new-looking rough road (a route for vehicles bound for the sand and gravel working away to the left) and immediately ahead, by a triple footpath sign is a stile. Cross, and immediately turn left along the edge of the field, a barbed wire fence and a hedge on the left. The hedge soon veers away to the left but the path goes on, straight ahead.

Cross a stony track and carry on by the path ahead, across a field and come to another footbridge over White Brook. Then immediately turn left after crossing the bridge and soon a path comes in from the right, merging with ours. Do not change direction and soon cross the Brook by yet another bridge.

Next comes a stile and, at a footpath sign the path bends right to skirt sand and gravel workings to the left. They are not picturesque, but quite interesting. As it bends left the path becomes pebbly and then, beyond a stile, you should bear right into a residential road (Summerleaze Road) at a corner and turn left. Half a mile of residential road walking lies ahead, unfortunately (but unavoidably), until you reach Boulter's Lock. Summmerleaze Road bends right and comes to a crossing road (Sheephouse Road) at which you turn right and then to a crossroads at which you turn left (Ray Mill Road East). This soon meets the main road (A4094) on the other side of which is the river Thames, Boulter's Lock and an elegant balustraded bridge linking with an island where pleasure grounds offer a delightful place to rest.

The walk continues along the road, the river on the right, for a short distance beyond the lock until you leave the road where the towpath diverges from it. The river looks narrow here but this is because you are still walking level with the island, which is quite big. When you have passed its tip, however, and the water has widened out, the most glorious views of the Cliveden woods open up; thick woods with trees of many kinds like a great green cliff rearing out of the water.

Just beyond the last of the rather grand riverside houses on the left you cross – positively for the last time – the White

Brook, where it empties itself into the Thames. There is still some way to go along this lovely stretch of the walk before the great house, Cliveden Court, comes into view, dramatically perched high on the hillside.

Eventually you will reach a point where, at the site of the strangely-named My Lady Ferry (the decaying remains of the old landing stage are still discernible), you can go no further beside the water. So here you must turn left to follow a clear path within a wood. Be a little careful when the path forks right to join a drive, for your route lies along the path's left fork, ahead. Again it forks, and again take the left fork. At the end of the path you will come to a stile by a footpath sign and then, on the other side of a drive, to another sign pointing to a 'Public Footpath', a broad path which brings you out into Mill Lane where you turn left. This peaceful lane skirts a cricket field and comes out eventually to the A4094.

Now you can either take the quiet School Lane opposite, which by-passes Cookham's main street, or turn right for a couple of hundred yards and then left at the Stanley Spencer Gallery into the High Street if you want to sample the village's fleshpots: the tea rooms, restaurants and pubs with which it is generously endowed, and the shops. Whichever route you take we shall meet by the war memorial – and what a tragically long 1914–18 list of names it bears for such a little place. The car park is only a short distance ahead, on the right.

Historical Notes

Boulter's Lock: I suppose Boulter's Lock is always called the most famous lock on the river because it is so easy to get to, lying as it does beside a main road. On a summer day it is thronged with people, as it was in Edwardian days when it was **the** fashionable boating centre. 'Boulter' is a name for a miller and an old flour mill still stands on the island. It was built in 1726 but converted to an inn in 1950. The first lock to be constructed here was built around the end of the 18th century, the first of the first eight. The present lock, however, dates from just before the First World War. It is slightly unusual in that the lock chamber is provided with an intermediate set of gates so that when traffic is light, time and water can be saved by using only part of the chamber.

Cliveden Court: The original house, only parts of which still stand, was built by George Villiers, 2nd Duke of Buckingham, a favourite of Charles II. After a great fire in 1795 it was rebuilt and occupied by the Duke of Sutherland. Another fire destroyed this second house in 1849 after which the building as we see it today was built to the design of Sir Charles Barry, the architect of the Houses of Parliament. It was subsequently bought by William Waldorf Astor, an American millionaire whose wife, Nancy Lady Astor, was the first woman to be elected to Parliament, in 1919. Lord Astor gave the estate to the National Trust in 1942 and the house is now let as an hotel.

For information about Cookham and the Stanley Spencer Gallery see the notes following Walk Eight.

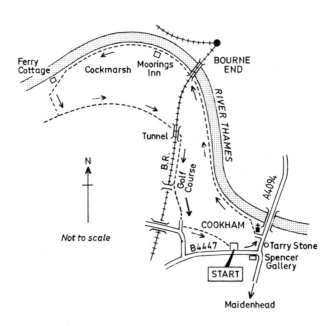

Ferry
Cottage

Cockmarsh

Moorings
Inn

BOURNE
END

RIVER THAMES

Tunnel

B.R.

Golf
Course

A4094

N

Not to scale

COOKHAM

B4447

START

Tarry Stone

Spencer
Gallery

Maidenhead

Cookham

Introduction: A varied ramble with only some gentle gradients that won't trouble anyone. There are many pleasant views to be enjoyed, not only on our 2 mile walk beside the river but on the return route to Cookham where, from a high point, we obtain what is undoubtedly the finest prospect of the day. Cookham, birthplace of the artist Stanley Spencer, is a most attractive and interesting village and you will find it well worth while to spend a little time there, either before or after your walk. You may also visit The Stanley Spencer Gallery.

Distance: The circuit of about 3¾ miles can be comfortably completed in a couple of hours.

Refreshments: Cookham itself is well supplied with pubs, restaurants and tea rooms. About a third of the way round the circuit is the riverside Moorings Inn, where food may be obtained, while at the appropriate time of year a van selling ice creams and soft drinks is usually stationed on the car park where the walk starts and finishes.

How to get there: The walk starts in the small, free car park on Cookham Moor, the same starting point as for the previous walk. Cookham village is on the A4094 which runs north from Maidenhead towards Bourne End, and Cookham Moor is reached by turning west onto the B4447 in the village. The car park lies on the right-hand side, a short distance beyond the last of the buildings. (OS sheet 175, GR 893 853).

The Walk: Walking on the Moor, make your way back to the village, past the war memorial and along the High Street, which contains some lovely old buildings; note particularly the splendid Bel and Dragon Hotel, one of the country's oldest licensed establishments. On coming to the main road, turn left in the direction signposted to Bourne End and Wooburn. First, however, you will observe the Stanley Spencer Gallery, housed in a former Methodist chapel. There is something else of interest to see before you go much further – the Tarry Stone, on the other side of the road. A meterorite, maybe.

Almost at once, turn left into Church Gate, signposted 'Church', and enter the churchyard, taking the good path past the west end of the church and thankfully noting that the forefathers of the village are resting in peace and not resurrecting as in Spencer's most famous picture. Holy Trinity church was one of his favourite subjects. Due to the weight of the roof the north and east walls are leaning outwards but as they have been doing so for 800 years they will doubtless stand up until after your visit.

Through a kissing gate you come to the Thames and turn left. The first few hundred yards are park-like and the boats moored along the water's edge contribute to a lively scene. Passing Cookham Reach Sailing Club's premises you are then in open country. Your way is along the towpath for nearly 2 miles, so ignore the signposted footpath running left just before an odd little bridge that seems to do no more than allow water from the river to supply a drinking pool for cattle.

Cross a stile almost opposite Andrew's Boathouses and enter Cockmarsh, a wide open space owned by the National Trust, where you will find the path ahead shaded by a long line of trees, many of them ancient willows with curiously riven trunks. Pass under a railway bridge and the scene changes again. Boats are moored on either side of the river and, on your side, there are a number of bungalows. And then – the Moorings Inn with its riverside bar inviting a stop.

A few more dwellings are passed before a gate leads back into open country once more. Another gate and a little bridge bring you to a path beside a very large field with trees interposed between path and river. You may observe, as you pass it on the right, the remains of a now quite useless gate, apparently indicating that the towpath, with the passage of time, has moved itself a few feet inland; the result of bank erosion, presumably.

Soon you will arrive at Ferry Cottage, a pretty white-painted house. The ferry, of course, has long gone, so there is no way of reaching the towpath which continues on the other bank. Our towpath walk ends here, therefore, but happily a path continues leftish across a field towards a double footpath sign. Turn left on reaching it and cross the field towards a wooded hill ahead. At the end of the field you will find a stone stile. Cross it and go forward to a clear, wide track running from right to left. Turn left upon it, ignoring at least six other small paths going off in all directions. Your route is on the level, at the base of the hill, on what was pretty obviously a railway track many years ago.

Eventually, you will reach a high stile and, after negotiating it, the path lies ahead along a tree-lined way towards a little railway bridge. Pass beneath the railway and cross a stile on the right. Go left for a few yards, then up a flight of steps on the right, which leads to a golf course.

The path skirts to the right of the golf course and climbs gently, then levels out, then rises up a steep, but short, slope to a bridge over the railway. Pause here, for from this vantage point you get the best view of the day, a panorama of the river. It looks even lovelier from here than it did from the towpath, with glorious wooded hills behind.

Do not cross the bridge, but take the path – which is invisible on the ground – slightly left across the grass, heading towards the left-hand end of the right-hand group of trees ahead. Then, with the path now fairly clear and with wire fencing on the right, you come to a stile and cross it. Two drives lie ahead and you should take the left-hand one in a forward direction until, just before reaching a narrow road, you turn left down a path by a house called 'Fiveways'; the path runs to the right of a track which heads towards a wooden field gate. The path is straight and narrow and ends at a stile.

Cross the stile and go half right beside a willow-lined stream. The path reaches a stile and, beyond it, a rough concrete bridge spans the stream. The path then leads on through the bushes and comes out in the car park where you left your car.

Historical Notes

Cookham was known to the Romans as a place where the river could be forded and Domesday Book describes it as already a market town. A special atmosphere is bestowed by Cookham Moor. Lying at the end of the High Street, it is owned by the National Trust and, being of 9 acres, is vastly bigger than the usual village green.

Holy Trinity church, probably on the site of a Saxon church, blends Norman, Early English and Perpendicular styles. Its splendid late Perpendicular tower is a landmark for miles around. Of particular note is an unspoilt Norman window, quite small, in the north wall. A 15th century memorial to the Babham family is worthy of notice, as is another to a later member of the family, with his wife and six children. Also in the church may be seen an excellent copy of one of Sir Stanley Spencer's enigmatic paintings, of the Last Supper.

Cookham's Victorian bridge, although built very cheaply, is quite pleasing and the toll cottage really did house a toll collector until as recently as 1947 when the local authority took it over and tolls were no longer levied.

The Tarry Stone, possibly a meteorite, which is displayed near the road junction at one end of the High Street, has played a part in Cookham village life for a long time for it is known that country sports were held around it more than 500 years ago, on Cookham Moor.

Although it has associations with Charles II and Nell Gwynne, the name that most readily springs to mind when

Cookham is mentioned is that of Sir Stanley Spencer, one of the best-known painters of the 20th century. He was born in the village in 1891, in a house in the High Street called 'Fernlea'. The Stanley Spencer Gallery, housed in a former chapel on the corner of the High Street is unique as the only gallery in Britain devoted exclusively to an artist in the village where he was born and spent most of his working life. He is especially noted for paintings of Christ in a modern English setting. The gallery contains a permanent collection of Spencer's work, together with letters, documents and memorabilia. It also displays important works on long-term loan and mounts a winter and summer exhibition each year.

The gallery contains the pram in which the artist wheeled his equipment and materials when painting around the parish church, the High Street Cookham Moor and the river.

The Stanley Spencer Gallery is open daily from Easter to October from 10.30am to 5.30pm, including weekends, and on Saturday, Sunday and Bank Holidays from November to Easter from 11am to 5pm.

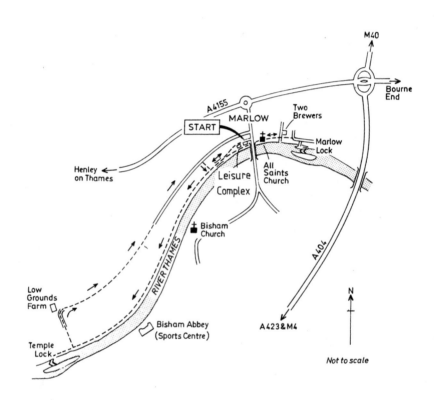

Marlow

Introduction: A gentle walk with no gradients or difficulties. 'Blotted his copybook' – a familiar saying, the origin of which we shall discover today! We shall see two lovely locks and a pleasant town full of delightful Georgian buildings and with one of the Thames' most famous bridges. The stretch of the river beside which we walk is very pleasant. Bisham Abbey on the other side of the water, with its ghostly legend contributes a special fascination to the journey.

Distance: A circuit of about 4 miles. I would allow 2½ hours if I were you, especially as you will probably wish to spend a little time watching the boats go through Temple and Marlow locks.

Refreshments: Marlow itself, of course, offers facilities of every kind. Towards the end of the circuit will be found a refreshment kiosk by the children's play area near Marlow church.

How to get there: Marlow lies on the A4155 which runs from Henley-on-Thames to Bourne End. The town can also be conveniently reached from Junction 9 on the M4 and along the A423 and A424, or from Junction 4 on the M40. Park in the car park in Pound Lane, adjoining the Court Gardens Leisure Complex. Pound Lane runs west from a mini-roundabout on the town side of the bridge. (OS sheet 175, GR 849 861).

The Walk: Leave the car park by walking towards the cricket field and then bear left, keeping to the right of some iron railings until you reach the tow path and then make towards a small bridge on the right and cross it.

Before long you will pass, on the other side of the river, Bisham's charming little waterside church with its 12th century tower. Cross a wooden footbridge over a tributary stream and, soon afterwards, another little bridge. Beyond this point wide views to distant hills open up ahead and to the right and left.

The next point of interest on the opposite bank is Bisham Abbey. In his younger days, Henry VIII – who built it – was a noted athlete so he would probably have enjoyed what goes on there today for it is a Sports Council Centre for physical recreation. You may well see a variety of activities in progress over there.

Another little bridge takes you over another stream. Go through a gate beside a cattle grid and, shortly, observe a tiny memorial to a long-serving Honorary Secretary and Treasurer of Marlow Amateur Regatta and his wife, facing the Regatta's course. On coming abreast of Temple Island, cross another bridge and then the weirs of Temple lock come into view and within earshot.

Just before you come level with the first weir a stony track leads off to the right. You will turn along here – but, first, go a little further beside the river for a closer look at picturesque Temple lock with its flower beds in a setting of chestnut trees and to go onto the new footbridge, for a lovely view.

The track, to which you return, comes to a tubular metal gate and then runs straight ahead between fields towards Low Grounds Farm. Just short of the farm, where the main track bends right then left, a rougher track goes off to the right. This is the way to go. The clear track runs, between wire fences, along the right-hand edge of a large field.

At the end of the field cross a stile and find the path continuing through woodland before transforming itself into an asphalt lane which soon crosses a concrete bridge. On reaching a rough layby on the right turn right along a narrow and shady path. This leads back to the riverside where you turn left to enjoy, after the river has curved a little, a good view of Marlow's famous suspension bridge. Soon, the little bridge where you started your towpath walk is reached and the way back to the car park is, as you will remember, on the path to the left. But I would like you to come first on a short, yet very interesting, walk to Marlow lock through fascinating Seven Corner Alley.

Carry on beside the river until the path forks and then go left. Cut across the grass towards an iron gate leading into the road almost opposite All Saints' church (unless you want to divert, first, a few yards across the grass to the refreshment kiosk you will notice beside the children's play area.)

Cross the road and go to the left of the churchyard wall until, just past the stone gateposts (the gates are missing) a small path signposted 'Marlow lock' will be found. The path curves left, now between walls, to emerge facing The Two Brewers, one of Marlow's most notable pubs. On the right-hand side of it the path, again signposted to 'Marlow lock', continues between walls. The narrow path you are following was used by bargemen to bring their towing horses from the lock to Marlow bridge. In those days, as now, there was no towpath between these points, in consequence of which a long towing line and a complicated system of winches were needed.

You will come out into a quiet residential road and turn right for a few yards to the river, where the road bends left and a 'Public footpath' sign points the way over a bridge to the lock. I think you will agree that the memorable view from the bridge – of river, weir, suspension bridge and church – makes this short diversion well worth while and is an ample reward for the necessity now to retrace your steps to the car park.

Historical Notes

Marlow is a pleasant little town, particularly noted for its Georgian houses the most noted of which is Marlow Place, built in 1720 and lived in by the Prince of Wales, later George II. All Saints' church, of brick and stone, was rebuilt in 1834 and altered in 1870. It replaced a much older church greatly damaged by flooding. Inside are a number of monuments much older than the present building. One is a wall monument to Sir Miles Hobart, a Speaker of the House of Commons, who was killed in 1636 when his coach overturned, a calamity which a bas-relief on the monument depicts.

The grave of John Richardson, a showman who was born in the town's workhouse, may be seen. Beside him lies 'The Spotted Boy', a young negro whom he brought from the Carribean and whom he exhibited throughout the country. But the English climate seemed not to have agreed with the unfortunate youngster who died, aged 8, in 1812. There is a portrait of the boy in the vestry.

Marlow's deservedly famous, graceful suspension bridge, opened in 1836, was designed by William Tierney Clark. Fame has largely eluded this unlucky bridge-builder for his Hammersmith Bridge was replaced in 1887 while his most notable work, the bridge that linked Buda with Pest, was destroyed in the Second World War.

Bisham: The church, largely rebuilt in the 19th century, retains its 12th century tower and a 16th century chapel. Among the numerous interesting monuments is one to Lady Elizabeth Hoby and her seven children. An aunt of Francis Bacon, she lived in nearby Bisham Abbey and is said to have become so enraged with her clumsy and mentally-retarded son that she beat him to death for blotting his copybooks. Oddly enough, some badly blotted and bloodstained 16th century copybooks were found in an attic by workmen renovating the Abbey some years ago, which seems to lend support to the legend. No wonder Lady Elizabeth's remorseful ghost haunts the Abbey still.

Originally founded in the 12th century for a community of Knights Templar (hence nearby Temple Lock), the well-preserved Tudor house was built by Henry VIII after the earlier building was destroyed at the Dissolution of the Monasteries. The king gave it to his fourth wife, Anne of Cleves who, in turn, exchanged it with the Hoby family for a manor in Kent. Sir Thomas Hoby was custodian of the young Princess Elizabeth and kept her here for three years during the reign of her half-sister, Mary.

The priory church, destroyed at the Dissolution, housed the tomb of Warwick the Kingmaker, who was buried here in 1471. Other famous warriors rested there, too.

Materials from the abbey went into the construction of the present house, the porch and great hall being now the oldest parts of the building.

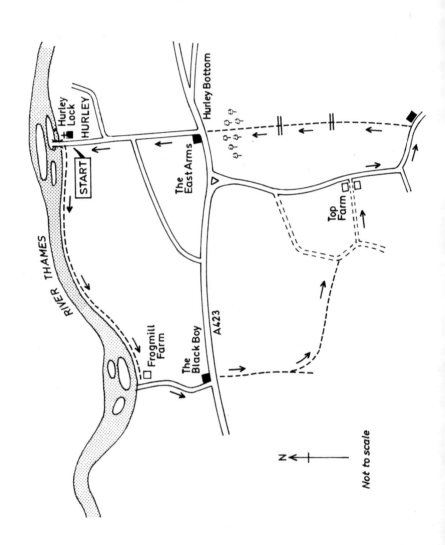

RIVER THAMES

Hurley Lock

HURLEY

START

The East Arms

Hurley Bottom

Top Farm

Frogmill Farm

The Black Boy

A423

N

Not to scale

Hurley

Introduction: This is an enjoyable ramble through pleasant countryside with easy gradients apart from one which, although fairly steep, is in a downward direction. There is the interesting church at Hurley to be visisted, some good views and a woodland glade to be enjoyed along the way. A couple of paths on this walk might be found slightly over-grown at certain seasons of the year, so I do recommend trousers to protect your legs against stinging nettles.

Distance: The ramble covers about 5¼ miles. It can be completed comfortably in 2¾ hours.

Refreshments: The Black Boy is reached rather less than a third of the way round – and at the end of the 'easy' (the all-on-the-same-level) part. There are no further refreshment facilities until the final ¾ mile when you pass The East Arms, The Rising Sun, The Olde Bell, the village post office and the village store, together offering a wide variety of food, ice cream and drinks.

How to get there: The starting point is Hurley, a village lying at the end of a minor road, signposted 'Hurley Village', which runs north by the side of a pub called The East Arms on the A423 about 4 miles east of Henley-on-Thames. Drive down this minor road as far as you can and park in a large, free car park on your left. (OS Sheet 175, GR 825 840).

The Walk: The walk begins along a footpath, with a 'No Cycling' sign, beside the vehicle entrance to the car park. You may, however, first like to visit the nearby church of St Mary the Virgin, an interesting-looking flint edifice with a wooden tower. To the left of the church is the gateway to the former monastery, now private property, while the fine old Olde Bell Inn, which you undoubtedly noticed as you passed it in the car just now, is said to have been the monastery's guest house.

The path leads to a flight of steps leading to a wooden footbridge. Go up the steps but do not cross the bridge, although it is worth going onto it for the view of nearby Hurley Lock. At the top of the steps turn left to the Thames towpath. For the next few hundred yards the sound of water tumbling over the weirs comes across loudly from the other side of the river.

Step up onto, across and down from a small bridge and at once the views open up. Level with the far end of the weirs, pass through a gate by a cattle grid and continue on the gravelled path (which soon peters out, leaving us walking on grass). Keep fairly near the water's edge and after a while cross a stile the pattern of which will probably be as unfamiliar to you as it was to me.

Further along, a drive comes in from a caravan site on the left and an iron gate lies ahead. Pass by it and continue on a small path at the waterside. The river broadens now to embrace three luxuriant islands and you pass another iron gate to continue along a riverside drive. Ignore a 'Public Footpath' sign pointing left and soon, beyond double iron gates, a path goes right to follow the river more closely. Turn left after a few yards to join a pleasant, narrow country road to the right of, seemingly, farm buildings converted to dwellings (Frogmill Farm).

In ¼ mile the A423 is reached, at a pub called The Black Boy. Turn left for a few yards only and at the end of The Black Boy's buildings cross this busy, and fast, road carefully to a bridleway going up through the bushes. This is your way and this is the first of the paths that may be found a little over-grown. As it gently climbs, pleasant pastoral views open up. Ignore a permitted path going right, up the bank, to a wooden gate.

At the top of the hill carry on along the path ahead. Before long, two stone direction signs, close to the ground, will be encountered on the left, one of them indicating 'Public Bridle-way to Honey Lane'. Take this route, through a truly delightful woodland glade which is a nature reserve. Ignore a stile passed on the right, and leave the nature reserve by a wooden gate shortly afterwards.

Beyond this, the path soon becomes a cart track with wide views to be enjoyed to the right. The track merges with a concrete drive sweeping in from private property on the left but continue ahead with a wire fence on the right until a fenced cart track comes in from the left – just before the drive curves slightly right towards a wood. Turn squarely left onto the cart track towards Top Farm which can be seen ahead.

Bear right through the farm (it is a public right of way) and come out into a lane. Turn right here and at a T-junction turn left.

Just before reaching some red-brick houses cross a stile on the left. The path here is not discernible on the ground but it runs towards a stile near the far left-hand corner of the field. The path beyond the stile brings you to two plank bridges in close proximity and then to another stile. In the field on the other side of it the path may again not be plain on the ground but the way ahead is straight through the middle of the field to another stile on the far side of it. Cross a concrete drive, over a kind of stile, and along a wide, grassy path towards the centre of the wood ahead. You will first come to a stile with footpath signs beside it. Cross a drive and a stile and take the path ahead through another large field, still making for the wood.

Cross a stile and enter the wood and take the path with a wire fence on the left. The wood, although wide, turns out not to be deep and before long you are at a stile which leads to a path going straight ahead, quite steeply downhill. This path, too, may be found slightly overgrown, especially towards the end.

At the end of the path you come out, over a stile at Hurley Bottom, onto the A423 again. Cross the road carefully and take the minor road through Hurley village, passing (or not passing!) The East Arms, The Rising Sun and The Olde Bell in the comparatively short distance before you reach your car.

Historical Notes

Hurley: Overlooking the small green is the church of St Mary the Virgin. The nave and chancel are long and narrow, yet when they formed part of the 11th century Benedictine priory they were twice as long. The church forms one side of a square in which remains of the monastic buildings can be glimpsed, including the refectory, now a private house. Two features to note within the church are a wooden cross, mounted high on the east wall above the altar, which is believed to be one of the oldest wooden crosses in England; the other is the Lovelace Memorial, erected about 1605. Two Elizabethan gentlemen kneel face to face; they are Richard Lovelace who was Lord Lieutenant of Berkshire and Constable of Windsor Castle, and his son Sir Richard Lovelace. At some time the chancel floor was raised, completely burying the inscription at the base of the monument. Further monastic remains of Hurley Priory are an old tithe barn in the village street and a 14th century dovecote nearby. Irene Vanbrugh, an actress whom older readers will remember, is buried in the churchyard.

Medmenham

Introduction: This most rewarding walk includes an uphill stretch of the legs, worth it for the views. It then passes through deep woodlands, always places of special atmosphere. The riverside part of the ramble has glorious views on either side – a mile and a half of sheer delight by a lovely reach of the Thames.

Distance: The circuit is about 8 miles and the time required about 3¾ hours.

Refreshments: There are no refreshment facilities on the actual circuit but a diversion may be made to the ancient Dog and Badger in Medmenham; ⅔ mile there and back. Bar meals are offered.

How to get there: At Mill End, about 3 miles from Henley-on-Thames on the A4155 towards Marlow, a minor road sign-posted 'Hambleden, Skirmett and Fingest' runs north. A quarter of a mile along this road, on the left, is a free car park. This is our starting point. (OS sheet 175, GR 785 855).

The Walk: Leave the car park and turn right for a few yards only to a minor road on the left and immediately go left through a swing gate. The path follows the left-hand edge of the field and comes, after about ⅓ mile, to a swing gate leading into a rough lane just short of a little bridge. Cross the bridge and keep left when the lane forks.

Look out for a gap in the hedge on the right after approximately ¼ mile, where a waymarked path begins. Follow this

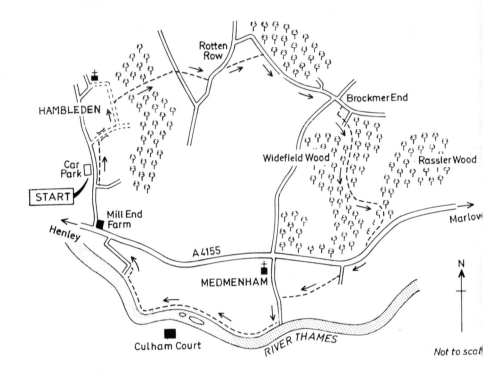

path up the hill and through the wood, climbing all the way – but before entering the wood glance over your right shoulder at a truly beautiful view. Keep to the main path through the wood, ignoring all minor paths left and right, until you meet a waymarked crossing track near the top of the hill. Turn left and, after only a few yards, go over a stile lying a short distance back from the path, on the right; be careful not to miss it.

The path then goes ahead, by the side of a wood at first and then straight across the field until stiles and gates are reached at either side of a crossing track. Beyond the second stile a grassy track leads to a narrow road in which you turn left.

Ignore a footpath sign you soon pass on the right and, when the road bends sharply left at a farm, carry on ahead by a footpath sign and through a metal gate on the other side of which the path – not very visible here – runs straight ahead over the field to a stile. Over this, and still keeping to the 'invisible' path go over the field to another stile you will soon see plainly against the dark trees behind it. Over the stile, and over a gate, you are in a very pleasant leafy lane, where you turn right.

Keep to the lane for 10 minutes or so and at a junction of little roads by Brockmer End Farm carry on for a short distance on the road ahead. At a footpath sign on the right just past a house called Widefield, a short length of path (over-grown maybe) takes you to a stile on the left. Cross it and go slightly right over a field to a stile near its far right corner. Cross a concrete drive (half right) to a stile leading into Widefield Wood.

Now be a little careful. After 16 paces there is a kind of junction of paths but your path goes forward slightly then bears rightwards. Waymarks (white painted arrows on the trees) will guide you all the way through this dark and, some may say, eerie wood; I only wish the waymarks were more plentiful near the beginning and around the middle. Eventually you leave the wood by a stile.

The path then curves slightly and comes to a stile leading into a rough track. Opposite, another stile brings you into another wood. There are only a few waymarks to guide you now but the path, which keeps very near to the right-hand edge of the wood, is plain enough. It climbs for a while and, towards the end bends left and comes out into a drive in which you turn left to the A4155.

Turn right. There is now an unavoidable, but short, stretch of road walking although there is a sidewalk of sorts for most of the way and it is downhill. Follow, after about ⅓ mile, a footpath sign on the left pointing down a drive to Abbey Lodge. Over a small bridge, an iron gate on the right marks the start of a path to a stile. Beyond, the path across the field is sometimes quite invisible, which makes the instruction on a nearby notice board, 'Keep Strictly to Footpath' easier to say than to obey. Nevertheless, if you head towards the left-hand side of a low wooden building you can see in the distance, you won't go far wrong.

Over a stile, and then another stile and a wooden footbridge, a clear path runs ahead at the right-hand edge of a wood. It leads out to a pleasant small road by Monks Cottage at Medmenham. It is from this point that you can, if you wish, divert to the right to the 14th century Dog and Badger; a diversion of ⅔ mile, there and back.

The walk proper, however, goes to the left and before crossing the small footbridge and going right, along the tow-path, just the barest glimpse may be obtained over the wall to the left of the pseudo ruin of Medmenham Abbey. No sooner will you have started walking along the towpath than you will see an elaborate monument recording the happy outcome of what was evidently a prolonged legal battle. Somebody must have been pleased with the result to have commissioned such a costly erection. The plaque reads: 'This monument was erected to commemorate the successful action fought by Hudson Ewe-bank Kearley, 1st Viscount Devonport PC, which resulted in the Court of Appeal deciding on the 28th March 1899 that Medmenham Ferry was public.' Alas, there has been no ferry at all these many years, public or private.

A mile and a half of sheer delight lie ahead. This is indeed a lovely reach of the river, with glorious views on either side. There is little, however, for me to point out to you apart from Culham Court, a splendid red brick mansion of 1770 which you will not fail to notice on the opposite bank anyway. I will therefore leave you to enjoy your towpath walk until it is cut off abruptly by the garden of a white, thatched house. Turn right here and make your way beside a hedge up the left-hand side of a field at the end of which there is a stile on the left leading into a drive. Carry on ahead along this long, straight drive to the A4155 road.

Turn left for a short distance and, just past Mill End Farm, turn right into the road in which the car park lies.

Historical Notes

Medmenham Abbey: You need actually to be on the river for a proper sight of Medmenham Abbey; all you can obtain from your viewpoint on land is a glimpse over a high wall.

What seems to be a ruin is, in fact, an 18th century folly built with materials from the demolished Cistercian monastery founded in 1204. The house on the site, partly Elizabethan and later extended, was occupied in the 18th century by Sir Francis Dashwood. Here it was that he and the other eleven members of an aristocratic sect calling themselves 'The Hell Fire Club' met regularly in the mid 1700s. What diabolical debauchery they got up to, dressed in fantastic vestments, is uncertain but was probably not so squalid as legend has it. Certainly these young bloods all settled down to respectable and useful careers later on. One of them was John Wilkes who, despite being expelled from the House of Commons for his critical writings about the government, became a notable champion of Parliamentary reform.

Hambleden, although not directly on our circuit, is recommended for a visit by car after the walk. Simply turn left out of the car park for about a mile and fork right into the village.

You will find it a charming, quite unspoilt place with its flint and brick cottages in a triangle around the village pump. The church has been gracefully adorned by several memorial gifts of fittings and furnishings in recent times. It contains some interesting older memorials, particularly an elaborate monument to the 17th century Sir Cope D'Oyley, his wife and ten children. Two of his sons tragically found themselves on opposing sides during the Civil War.

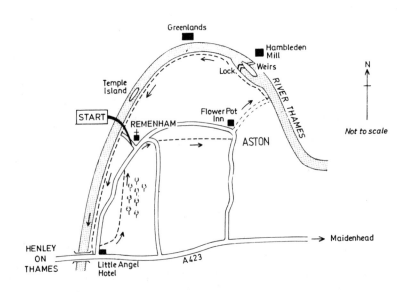

Remenham and Henley

Introduction: This is one of my favourite walks. It is a pleasant walk through wide fields and meadows, along an attractive reach of the river with a sight of picturesque old Hambleden Mill, an adventurous expedition across turbulent weirs as an optional extra and – for those undertaking the longer walk – a little something that will surely bring a lump to the throat of any dog lover.

However, I would not recommend that you attempt the walk during the period of Henley Royal Regatta. Not only are the roads around Henley-on-Thames likely to be congested at that time but part of the towpath between Remenham and Henley then ceases to be a public right of way so only the shorter walk of 3 miles may be undertaken. Moreover, parking may not be permitted during this period by Remenham church, which is where our walk commences. You could, however, try to park near the river at the end of the road beside the Flower Pot Inn in Aston village and start (and finish) the walk from the fourth paragraph of 'The Walk' section, below. But, on balance, I would wait until the Regatta was over if I were you.

Distance: The whole circuit is 5¼ miles. The shorter walk omitting the towpath length to Henley bridge and back to Medmenham through woods and fields, is 3 miles. About 2¾ hours walking-time should be sufficient for the full circuit, including the optional trip over the weirs at Hambleden lock.

Refreshments: The Flower Pot Inn in Aston village offers snacks. The Little Angel Hotel, by Henley bridge, provides bar food, too, but by diverting a short distance over the bridge into Henley refreshment facilities of almost every kind may be found. A van selling ice creams and soft drinks is usually stationed by Hambleden lock on summer days.

How to get there: The hamlet of Remenham can be reached down either of two small signposted roads running north from the A423. One of them, Remenham Lane, leaves the main road just to the east of Henley bridge by the Little Angel Hotel. The other, which you will come to first if you are approaching from the London/Maidenhead direction, is signposted 'Remenham Church' and it leaves the A423 the second turning after the main road begins its steep descent down Remenham Hill into Henley. It should not be difficult to park near Remenham church. (OS sheet 175, GR 771 842).

The Walk: Remenham church is dedicated to St Nicholas. There has been a church here since before 1066 but 19th century restorations, alas, eliminated most of the ancient building. You will probably find it locked.

Start the walk by taking the road to the right of the church and when it soon forks, take the right fork. The road climbs quite steeply for a while, giving good views over the wide meadows to the river and to Temple Island and then it curves to the right. At the end of the curve a track, signposted 'Public Footpath' goes off to the left. Follow this track, with great rolling fields on either side.

Now be a little careful. At the point where the track turns sharply left and becomes a rough lane, go ahead by a tiny path. The first few yards may be somewhat overgrown. Follow the rather faint path through a field and come out, over a stile, into a small road by Highway Cottage in Aston village. Turn left down the road to the Flower Pot Inn. Take the road to the right of the inn. Ignore a 'Public Footpath' sign you pass on the left and soon you reach the river.

Turn left over a footbridge and proceed with the river on

your right. There is, for the most part, no path to speak of but you can't go wrong. After a short ½ mile the famous white weather-boarded 16th century Hambleden Mill, which worked until 1958, will be seen on the opposite bank and, long before Hambleden lock comes into view, the sound of water tumbling over its weirs will have reached you. It's an impressive sight, you'll agree, when you get there.

You can, if you wish, go over to Hambleden Mill along a narrow footbridge which crosses the weirs. The rushing water beneath makes this quite an exciting experience. It is safe, although children, needless to say, must be kept under control.

When you return from your expedition across the weirs, continue the walk past the lock, still keeping to the riverside. The path, you will notice, changes its character from time to time being sometimes narrow, sometimes broad, occasionally made up and often invisible. You will pass, in a landscape adorned with decorative trees on the opposite bank, a beautiful house called Greenlands. Originally built in 1604, it was rebuilt in 1853 by a First Lord of the Admiralty, W H Smith, a member of the well known newsagents' family. It is now The Management College.

Then you come to luxuriant Temple Island which you saw in the distance soon after the start of the walk. At the far end of the island is a curious cottage with a cupola that gives the island its name.

Soon after passing the island you will reach a point where there is a low wall on the left, then a stile beside a wide double iron gate. **For the shorter walk**, cross the stile and take the walled lane the short distance to Remenham church.

For the longer walk, cross the stile adjoining a small cattle grid beside the river. The boathouses of Henley and the church tower beyond them can now be seen ahead. Ignore a footpath sign which you shortly pass, indicating a path leading away from your route, which continues at the waterside. You will pass the UTRC boathouse, the Remenham Club clubhouse and several footbridges and gates as you gradually approach Henley bridge. This is the reach of the river which comes alive during Henley's famous regatta week.

Just before Henley bridge by the Leander Club, the path swings away from the river and leads to the busy A423 road – but only for a few yards. Turn left and very shortly leave the main road by going left into quiet Remenham Lane beside The Little Angel Hotel. About 150 yards along it, just after passing the Home Farm entrance, a 'Public Footpath' sign points your way over a stile on the right. Follow the path towards a small gap in the trees ahead and then cross a stile and go half-left over a field, a waymark indicating the direction. At the far side a narrow path leads up through the trees.

Before entering this path, however, don't fail to pause and read the touching inscription on a small tablet erected to the memory of a much loved little dog named Minty who 'roamed these lovely fields ... waiting always at this place for his mistress ... Thank you, Minty, wherever you are. March 4th 1970'.

Cross the stile ahead and take the earth path leftwards through the trees. It goes between hawthorn bushes along a hillside and can be slippery in wet weather but it soon improves. When the hawthorn bushes end, continue with a fence on the left. Cross another stile and carry on with the fence still on the left. Cross yet another stile, by a gate, and then the path drops down into Remenham Lane. Turn right along this delightful leafy lane, with the river below on the left, and you will soon find yourself back by Remenham church, where the walk began.

Historical Notes

Henley-on-Thames: Graceful Henley bridge was built in 1787. The masks of Thamesis and Isis, which we see on either side of its central arch as we approach, are the work of a local sculptress, the Honourable Mrs Damer, who was a cousin of Horace Walpole, the 18th century writer.

A busy market town for seven centuries, Henley's wide streets provide an excellent shopping centre and have numerous interesting buildings to show. They include several inns, of various periods. The view up the street from the bridge towards the town hall, built to commemorate Queen Victoria's Diamond Jubilee, seems to form a picture of what everyone imagines as a typical English country town. Near the late Gothic church of St Mary, with its 16th century tower, is a row of almshouses endowed by the Bishop of Lincoln in 1547 and rebuilt in 1830. Nearby, too, is the 16th century Speaker's House, so called as the birthplace of William Lenthall, Speaker of the Long Parliament and one of the men who signed the death warrant of King Charles I. Charles I stayed at the Red Lion Hotel twice and the Duke of Marlborough stayed there from time to time while Blenheim Palace was being built. The much under-utilized Kenton Theatre is the fourth oldest in the country.

The first Oxford and Cambridge boat race was rowed in 1829 from Hambleden to Henley. (Cambridge, wearing not light blue but pink, lost.) Rowing continued during the following decade and the Regatta was established in 1839. Under the patronage of the Prince Consort it became 'Royal' in 1851. The Leander Club is perhaps the most famous rowing club in the world; membership, mainly of University oarsmen, is gained entirely by rowing prowess.

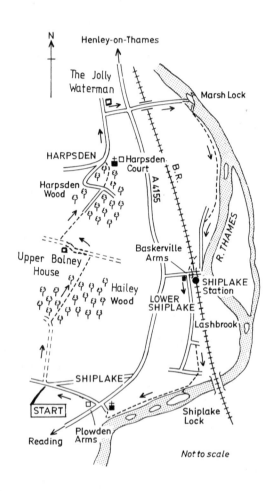

Shiplake

Introduction: 'In every English woodland you can hear the music of Delius', wrote Beverley Nichols. If that is so, you will hear his music today for our walk passes through several small, but very lovely, woods. This walk has a special attraction – the spectacular Marsh lock, curiously sited in the middle of the river. When one comes first to it, and starts across the causeway, the prospect is of breathtaking delight. On the debit side, however, there is perhaps a little road walking. It is unavoidable, but the roads are, for the most part, quiet country ones. If you have Ordnance Map sheet 175 and care to look at GR779796 you will see at once how much better this ramble would be if only the towpath were not interrupted at that point, for then you would be able to follow a most attractive stretch of the river and be spared a length of road.

One day, as the long-distance Thames Path becomes completed, the gap may be closed. At the time of writing, a wide unbridged drainage channel is the obstruction. But if, soon after you have passed the Baskerville Arms and are walking through Lashbrook, you see a new footpath sign, pointing left past the tiny, weatherboarded Lashbrook chapel, you will know that the path has at last been opened. So go that way; under the railay line and into the riverside meadows and follow the towpath to Shiplake lock and then pick up our route again from there.

Distance: This ramble covers 7 miles; 3½ hours should therefore comfortably cover the actual walking time.

Refreshments: Half way round is The Jolly Waterman; three-quarters of the way round is The Baskerville Arms; and at the end of the walk The Plowden Arms. All offer bar meals and snacks. Also, opposite The Baskerville Arms in Shiplake, is the well-stocked Corner Shop selling ice creams, cakes etc.

How to get there: The starting point is Shiplake, which lies on the A4155 Reading to Henley-on-Thames road about 2½ miles from the latter. Look out for a pub called The Plowden Arms and turn into a minor road signposted 'Binfield Heath and Peppard' beside it. There is another road similarly signposted but the one you want is the one alongside the pub. A little way along, on the right (just past a school) is Memorial Lane, signposted 'Henley'. Park in this road. Alternatively, you may be able to park in either of two small rough laybys on the left which you pass soon after turning at The Plowden Arms – then you won't have so far to walk at the end of the ramble. (OS sheet 175, GR760 785).

The Walk: Retrace your steps in Memorial Road and turn right and, after only a few yards, go right into a stony lane. It is very straight at first and bordered by trees, but when the lane eventually goes left carry on ahead along a cart track, with glorious views to the right.

After a while the track enters Hailey Wood. Keep to the main track running ahead and, shortly, downhill. Ignore all the tracks leading off on either side and keep always to the main one. The track ends when the wood ends. A path then runs clearly ahead across a field towards another wood, Harpsden Wood. (Head for a pair of posts bearing a power-line.)

Do not enter the wood yet. Instead, when you emerge at the end of the field into a drive, turn left along it. It soon narrows. At Upper Bolney House your way bends right, then left and continues beneath trees. Note the ha-ha in the garden on the left.

On coming to a stile on the right, just before the path divides, cross it and follow a path, half-right along the right-hand edge of the field to another stile. Another stile is now seen ahead across the next field and, over this, yet another in the corner of the field in front.

Across the last of these stiles, follow the stony lane opposite. Ignore all forks to the left and right and forge ahead on the main track until – be a little careful here – you reach a fork on the left signposted to 'Harpsden Wood House' and 'Harpsden Wood Cottage'. Here, bear half right onto a narrow, but waymarked, path through the woods. Cross a minor road and carry on along the waymarked path opposite, and directed by a signpost saying 'Footpath – Harpsden 1 mile'. It's a very short mile.

The path drops gradually towards the hamlet of Harpsden. The first things you notice there are the curious facings on three barns opposite the church. They are old wooden blocks formerly used in the printing of wallpaper.

After passing the church and the elegant entrance arch to Harpsden Court, bend left with the road, which begins as a pleasant country road but becomes residential later. However, it is not very far to Harpsden Park, a recent development of retirement homes; Henley War Memorial Hospital stood on the site when I came this way before. Immediately past it, turn right onto a bridleway which runs downhill and comes out into Waterman's Road, which leads ahead to the A4155. Here, if you wish, you can turn left for a few yards to The Jolly Waterman.

From Waterman's Road, cross, half-right, into Mill Lane. This goes past the Sports Centre, over a railway bridge and comes to the river Thames.

Now begins quite an exciting adventure. A long wooden cause-way take you over the swirling, white-frothed water that has tumbled over the weir and brings you to Marsh lock. No doubt you will wish to linger here for a while before setting off past the lock and across an even longer causeway which takes you back again to the side of the water from which you started. The towpath walk now begins.

This is a delightful reach of the river. You will notice from time to time some iron studs by the side of the path. They were put here in 1903 to mark the 14 ft width of the towpath but through bank erosion, caused by the wash from countless passing boats, the water's edge has crept very close to some of them. Near the end of the meadow, where the river splits into three channels, the towpath changes sides, but since the ferry has long gone you must leave the riverside for a while. A wooden footbridge leads to a stile and a path which crosses a rough track, then continues on the right of, but separate from, a drive.

When the footpath ends, carry on along the quiet private road ahead past some lovely houses with enchanting gardens and when the road forks, keep left. Opposite a house called Eyot Wood go half-right along a path (easily missed) between hedges and come to an iron kissing gate and a stile leading onto the railway. Cross carefully to the other side where a path leads up to a road junction at the Baskerville Arms.

Carry on along Mill Road opposite and through the hamlet of Lashbrook. (Remember what I wrote in the Introduction and look out for a sign that might be erected by the time you come this way, indicating that the length of towpath has been opened.) After about ½ mile, turn left into the drive of the British Red Cross Society's Andrew Duncan House. A few yards along, negotiate a steep stile on the right and cross the corner of a field to another stile. Turn right along the edge of a field and come out into a lane by picturesque Mill House. Turn right, then immediately left onto a footpath to Shiplake lock to reach the river again.

You can go over the footbridge to view the lock at close quarters if you wish, but return and cross the stile to the towpath. Another beautiful reach of the river lies ahead, a scene of tree-lined banks, tiny islands and sloping meadows. Over stiles, past Shiplake House, a white building high on the hill, and over a small footbridge the towpath walk leads eventually to a point below Shiplake College. Do not cross the substantial footbridge ahead but take the wide path which runs behind the boat-house (to which the water beneath the bridge gives access). Just where the path **almost** meets another path on the left, it curves round right, narrower here, and climbs to Shiplake church. Turn left (west) along the lane and come out to the A4155 almost opposite The Plowden Arms, near the starting point.

Historical Notes

Shiplake village is in two parts: the larger around the station and The Baskerville Arms, the smaller just a hamlet near the church of Saint Peter and Saint Paul. Although part of the church is 12th century it was heavily restored in the 19th. It is notable, however, for some brilliantly coloured 15th century stained glass from France brought, during the 19th century, from a ruined abbey in St Omer where it had lain buried since the French Revolution. Alfred, Lord Tennyson, was married here on 13th June 1850 and a poem (in my opinion not one of his best) which he wrote that day is on sale in the church. It is believed that the poem was accepted by the vicar in lieu of the wedding fee. In the churchyard may be seen numerous graves marking the resting places of members of the distinguished local family of Phillimore, eminent in the armed and civil services and the judiciary.

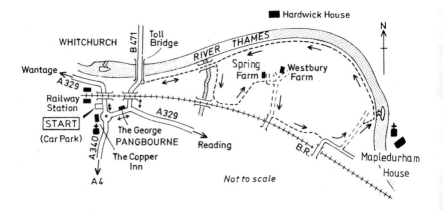

Pangbourne

Introduction: Mr Toad, Mole, Water Rat; these, and other, immortal characters from *The Wind in the Willows* must come to mind as we walk by the river at Pangbourne. For here is the birthplace of Kenneth Grahame, its author, who conceived these charming small animals who live and talk like humans. In other respects, too, this is a very pleasant, easy excursion, on paths that mostly range from good to excellent.

Distance: The circuit is 5½ miles; allow 2¾ hours.

Refreshments: None, I'm afraid, on the actual walk, but before or after you will find several pubs and cafés in Pangbourne.

How to get there: Pangbourne is on the A329 about 6 miles west of Reading. Our starting point is the public car park between The Copper Inn and the railway station. (OS sheet 175, GR633 765).

The Walk: At the roundabout in front of The Copper Inn take the road signposted 'Reading' and after a few steps turn into Whitchurch Road, by The George. Just before reaching the Victorian toll-bridge drop down right, through the Youth Services' car park, to the towpath and turn right. You are now on the National Trust's Pangbourne Meadow.

You are probably wondering why you are walking downstream when all the other walks in this book are upstream. The answer is that it is for only ½ mile or so and you will finish the walk on this same stretch of towpath in the 'proper' direction.

Cross two stiles and come to a small concrete footbridge over a tributary stream and another stile. Cross the stile and immediately turn right onto a path which runs beside the stream and keeps near it all the way to the railway embankment ahead; the path is not very visible until you have crossed, after about 100 yards, a stile. On reaching the railway embankment do not pass through the bridge under the line but turn left to follow a path running close to the foot of the embankment.

Neither should you go through another small railway bridge which is shortly reached but continue to maintain your direction beside the embankment. Soon the path bends left, with a wire fence on its right and pointing directly towards a smooth green hill in the distance ahead. The path turns right at the corner of the fence, passes to the right of Spring Farm and broadens out to become a wide grassy track with a sturdy wooden fence.

Having passed a double wooden gate, carry on along the farm road, turning right when it joins the lane from Westbury Farm. Immediately before the lane crosses the railway turn left along a path with a wire fence on either side and the railway below on the right. You may notice – indeed, you may well trip over them – some old iron boundary markers along the path with the inscription 'Great Western Railway Co's Boundary 1890'.

There is soon a bridge over the railway on the right and a triple footpath/bridleway sign on the left. Carry on ahead, maintaining the previous direction, but almost at once the path – now a bridleway – bears slightly left. It curves and eventually emerges into a road at a corner where you turn left along the road signposted 'Purley Village'. Just before the road ends, turn left along Mapledurham Drive at a 'Public Footpath' sign.

After passing an iron gate across your way, where the drive becomes a gravel track, you will pass a recreation ground called Bucknell's Meadow. When the track bends left, pass another gate then cross a field towards the weir which can be seen ahead.

On reaching the towpath, turn left through a gate to Maple-durham lock, a very attractive prize-winning lock, its flowerbeds a riot of colour. Pass beside it and out through a gate at the other end. Now begins a wholly delightful couple of miles of Thames-side walking. Look out for Hardwick House on the other side of the water.

You can put this book away now, if you like, for you cannot get lost. You will eventually come to the footbridge over the tributary stream which you crossed earlier and then you will know where you are. Follow the length of towpath through Pangbourne Meadow in the 'correct' direction this time, and then you will be back in the village where you left your car.

Historical Notes

Mapledurham: The great Elizabethan Mapledurham House near Mapledurham lock, is perhaps one of the finest Tudor houses in England. It was built in 1581 by Sir Michael Blunt who was Lieutenant of the Tower of London and remains in the hands of his descendants to this day. There are said to be secret rooms and passages inside, which were hiding places first for priests and later for Royalist soldiers during the Civil War. There has been a house on the site since before 1086.

St Margaret's church, near the house, is unusual in that an aisle in it remains Roman Catholic and is the burial place of members of the Blunt family. This section cannot be entered from the Anglican part.

The 15th century corn mill, on a site which housed a mill which is mentioned in Domesday Book, has been restored and is operational again. None of this can be visited as a diversion from our walk as the whole complex lies on the other side of the river and can only be glimpsed through the trees. But it is well worth making it the object of a special excursion. The house is open from Easter to the end of September; the mill for longer periods.

Hardwick House, of which we get a good view on our walk, was begun in the 14th century. It has been altered greatly several times since, notably after severe damage during the Civil War, but what we see is largely Tudor. Queen Elizabeth, 'tis said, slept here and Charles I, while a prisoner at Caversham Court, was permitted to come to play bowls.

Pangbourne is a charming village, but with little of historical note. Even the church of St James the Less, which is the most historically important building in the village, is largely Victorian. The present building (which at the time of writing is undergoing urgent, substantial repairs) is the third, if not the fourth church on the site since the first in the 12th century. The brick tower, dated 1718, remains from the previous church. There is a fine east window. Interesting tombs and memorial tablets, as well as the pulpit, from the previous building have been incorporated into the present one.

Goring

Introduction: This is one of our longer and more invigorating walks. It is very rewarding and our efforts in climbing the hills are repaid with some marvellous views – and one quite astonishing viewpoint. We start and finish in Goring, an attractive riverside village.

Distance: The circuit is about 8 miles; I took 3¾ hours.

Refreshments: The Queen's Arms, passed within a few minutes of the start of the walk, offers bar meals. No other refreshment places are encountered until you are back in Goring at the end of the walk, where there are pubs, restaurants and cafés. Half way round, the walk touches the fringe of Whitchurch, but to visit the nearest pub there, The Greyhound, would mean a diversion of about ⅔ mile, there and back.

How to get there: Goring may be reached from the A329, the Reading to Wallingford road, by turning onto the B4009 at Streatley and approaching the town across the bridge over the river; alternatively, by the B4526 or the B4009 from their junctions with the A4074, the Reading to Crowmarsh Gifford road. Follow the signs to the public car park. (OS sheet 175, GR600 806. This ramble strays off the edge of sheet 175 onto sheet 174, but there is no need to acquire that map.)

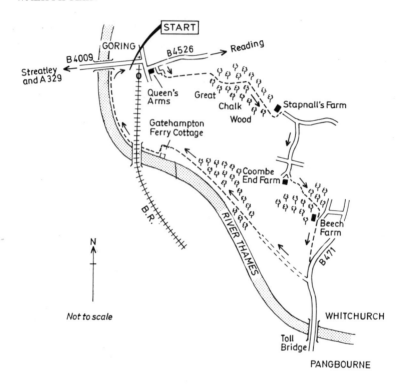

The Walk: Make your way to the bridge over the railway, at the end of the main street, and turn right into the Reading road (B4526) which starts just there. Turn left with it at The Queen's Arms. The second little road on the right is Whitehills Green. Enter it, go left as it bends, then right at the island and then along a hedged path to a stile. Go over a large, smooth playing field, half left, to a stile in its far corner.

Cross the stile and turn sharp left along the left-hand edge of the field. Here you must start climbing quite steeply but splendid views open up; glance over your right shoulder as you near the top. At a stile, the path flattens out but follow it still along the left edge of the next field. At the far corner of the field the path bends right and, in the next corner, cross another

92

stile and then, within a few yards, yet another which takes you into Great Chalk Wood.

Follow the clear path, which you may find a little overgrown at first. Ignore forks to the right and left through fire-breaks which you reach fairly soon, and carry on ahead. The path soon becomes a track and is not overgrown. When it bends to the left ignore an equally wide track from the right with which it merges and come to a good crossing track. Your way lies **ahead**, along a wide, shady track which later leads right when another track joins it from the left at a gate.

You may find this track, which climbs gently, a little muddy for a while. Near the top of the hill, at a T-junction of tracks turn left to a gate and carry on along the main path beyond the gate. The path soon ends at a field gate. Go through this gate and across the paddock to another gate, leading into a narrow lane. **Note:** By the time you read this, the path from the field gate to the lane may have been slightly diverted, but will still lead you to the lane.

To the left is Stapnalls Farm which, the farmer told me, stands on the site of a 13th century nunnery. Turn right along the lane and shortly go right into another lane which leads into a small road. The drive, opposite, is signposted 'Public Footpath, Whitchurch 1 mile' and this is the way to go. Follow the drive, bearing left when it forks and then, just short of the farm buildings, cross a stile on the left. The path, not very visible on the ground, skirts the buildings on the right and comes to a small, presently decrepit stile (part of which is an old tree trunk) on the right; it is easily missed, but it is immediately beyond the last of the farm buildings. Cross, and go half left across the field to a small stile in the barbed wire fence.

Now take your bearings so as to maintain your direction across the next field in which the path is quite invisible. But having lined yourself up in the same direction as you followed in the previous field, make towards the wood ahead and a stile leading into it.

Over the stile, the path through the wood goes **straight**

ahead. Ignore crossing paths and carry on ahead, the path weaving left and right a little at times. Go through an iron gate and a field and come out through another gate at Beech Farm.

Cross the drive and take a wide, grassy track which skirts the left-hand side of the farm. At the end of the buildings, your path jinks right, then left, then runs plainly, at first between hedges, before going forward at the right-hand edge of a field all the way to the B471 road. Turn right for a few steps to the Whitchurch war memorial – curiously isolated from the village – and cross the road. At this point an elevated path commences, which enables you to avoid walking on the road itself. When the path ends you will see a sign saying 'Public Bridleway, Goring 3 miles' and indicating a bridleway on the other side of the road. (Here, if you wish, you can carry on down the road into the village and to the pub, about ⅓ mile away.)

Go along the bridleway, which soon starts gently to climb. After a mile, when the main track turns sharply left to Hartslock Farm, go ahead on a footpath, a barbed wire fence on the right, and drop steeply down into a valley, then steeply up the other side. At a notice saying 'Private woodland. No shooting. Keep to arrowed path' enter a wood and, of course, the arrows painted on the trees make it difficult to lose your way.

Suddenly – delightful surprise – you find yourself at an astonishing viewpoint. You are on the edge of a cliff; the ground falls precipitously at your feet (there is a railing!) and there below is the Thames, an unexpected and breathtaking sight.

The path now runs along a wooded terrace high above the river with glorious views beyond it, and then begins slowly to descend. When the woodland ends the path continues with fields and hills to the right and the tree-lined river to the left.

Now be a little careful. You have to make your way to Gatehampton Ferry Cottage, on the riverside. The previous time I came this way there was some uncertainty as to the authorized route to it. There still is. Now, however, there is a new, clear path leaving the present path at a right angle, about

60 yards short of a white house ahead. Yet even this path is not waymarked, so you are advised to heed any new route signs, diversion signs or waymarks you may see.

At a tiny wooden footbridge by the cottage turn right onto the towpath. An overgrown section ends at a gate beyond which you pass beneath a railway bridge. You are now in the lovely Goring Gap where the Chilterns and the Berkshire Downs once probably joined, until the river bored and eroded a new way through for itself.

Carry on at the water's edge – although sometimes the path takes a short cut when the river meanders – and eventually you will reach Goring bridge, with Goring lock and weir behind. Turn right beside the bridge, past an old water mill and up onto the road. The Riverside Café is strategically placed just here. The other attractions of the village, and your car, are not far away.

Historical Notes

Goring and Streatley: The Thames between Goring and Streatley is wide and shallow and has been forded since early times. Settlements grew up on either bank, each with its nunnery. To this day, the name of Streatley seems always to be linked with that of Goring. The present bridge, that joins them, was built in 1923 and replaced a toll bridge.

Much remains of Norman construction in Goring's church of St Thomas of Canterbury and one of its bells has been calling villagers to worship for more than 600 years. The church, which contains some notable brasses, is believed to have been the chapel of Goring's nunnery, established in the 12th century. There are several picturesque buildings in the village, the most prominent of which is Ye Miller of Mansfield, a popular inn.

Streatley which, since the coming of the railway to Goring, has been (as it were) Goring's junior partner seems to have been the place of greater importance in former times. Long before the Romans came, and built a causeway over the river, a branch of the ancient Stone Age Icknield Way forded it. The Bull is a 16th century coaching inn. Like Goring's church, the church of St Mary the Virgin in Streatley is of Norman origin. Its tower is 15th century. Much restoration went on in Victorian times.

Streatley House, in the attractive High Street, is late 18th century and the village hall is interesting, being converted from former malt houses.